The Global Addiction to QE

An Investor's Guide to the Most Important
Topic Affecting Your Retirement

Michael J. Mattie

Consulting Editor
Jeanne M. Patrican

DWM Capital Press
Doylestown, PA

Michael J. Mattie
DWM Capital Press
165 West Ashland Street
Doylestown, PA 18901
www.dwmwealth.com

The Global Addiction to QE
1st edition, 2nd printing October 2016
Michael J. Mattie
ISBN 978-1-935355-19-9

Contents

Dedicated to my parents

John and Edna Mattie

*who epitomized the Greatest Generation.
The values they passed along remain
with the family today.*

I love and miss you both!

Prologue

Happiness comes when your work and words
are of benefit to yourself and others.

Buddha

Profound changes occurred in our financial system and economy as a result of the Great Recession of 2007 – 2009. Reflecting on the panic that engulfed our nation during this time, then US Treasury Secretary Timothy Geithner observed, "I thought we were looking at another global depression that would hurt billions of people." It was obvious to the financial elite on Wall Street that only unprecedented action would prevent a financial calamity from quickly escalating into an economic disaster.

This book explains the remarkable action taken to rescue our economy from the jaws of a global depression. Furthermore, it draws conclusions from the various forms of financial stimulus programs implemented over the past seven years to offer a glimpse of what the economic future may hold.

Quantitative Easing, QE for short, arrested falling stock markets and helped them lurch higher with each successive QE program. Even though this was the most important economic program initiated by the Federal Reserve, many investors don't know what QE is or how it affects the markets. Come to think of it, many *investment advisors* don't thoroughly understand Quantitative Easing and how it affects stock markets. The economic events that shaped our recovery from the Great Recession have been historic (as in "never happened in the history of our great country" kind of historic), and should be understood by investors preparing for, or in, their retirement years.

As I reveal the progression of QE throughout the book, it becomes apparent an addiction has engulfed our economy. An addiction to Quantitative Easing so intertwined with our banks, financial institutions, stock exchanges, Federal Reserve, US Treasury, pension funds, foreign central banks and investor retirement accounts, that I fear we have passed the point of no return, and unfortunately are *"Addicted to QE"* for a very long time. If not handled properly, attempts to wean us off this dependence and return to sustainable spending patterns will be met with dire consequences and the threat of a global depression.

When I began advising clients in 1991, things couldn't have been better for a rookie investment advisor. A surging stock market made it easy to employ basic asset allocation strategies as I engaged clients, gathered assets and thoroughly enjoyed my profession. Life was grand! Sure we had a downturn in stocks from 2000 – 2003, but the bull market continued until 2007, when the stock market unraveled and fell over 50% in just 17 months, stunning the vast majority of investors and advisors alike.

Several significant events converged in 2007 to cause a scary and seemingly uncontrollable plunge - most notably an over-leveraged US consumer unable to continue their spending and a financial system that ignored the warning signs of excessive risk taking. In response, the Federal Reserve was forced to stabilize the economy with Quantitative Easing, while the US Treasury and Congress simultaneously employed fiscal stimulus programs in their attempt to restore confidence. It was obvious to many this wasn't the 1990s anymore, with basic investing principles we learned now being questioned.

I struggled to grasp the true reason for the stock market recovery after the painful Great Recession, sifting through the clutter and noise of traditional financial media to locate the invisible hand that was guiding markets higher. It was becoming clear strategies that had worked for the past 50 years may have been hijacked by extreme measures taken to avoid a second great depression. QE appeared to be vital to the financial markets, so I endeavored to better understand it, the Fed and related topics. Even so, it was exceedingly difficult to guide my clients correctly because I was personally against the notion of QE, which essentially encouraged the creation of money out of thin air by banks and a quasi-government cartel called the Federal Reserve System, to stimulate the economy.

In the pages that follow, you will learn how stock markets were manipulated by the Federal Reserve using fiat currency (money not backed by a physical commodity). The Fed conjured over $3.6 trillion since the Great Recession (never in the history of our great country has this ever happened, not even close) and, unfortunately, more financial manipulation is expected.

Equally troubling, QE has become a global addiction. Commenting on China's explosive growth in the past six years, analyst Charlene Chu of Fitch Ratings (a prominent international credit rating agency) observed, "Most people are aware we've had a credit boom in China but they don't know the scale. At the beginning of all of this in 2008, the Chinese banking sector was roughly $10 trillion in size. Right now it's in the order of $24 to $25 trillion. That incremental increase of $14 to $15 trillion *is the equivalent of the entire size of the US commercial banking sector* (emphasis added) which took more than a century to build.

So that means China will have replicated the entire US system in the span of half a decade." She continued, "Mathematically, there is no way to grow out of this problem when credit is twice the size of the economy and growing twice as fast."

Financial advisors and investors who do not understand the fundamental relationship between the Fed's Quantitative Easing policy and its effect on the markets are putting investments at risk. The fundamentals of the stock market have changed, and investors need to understand this change in order to properly manage their investment portfolios.

The intent of this book is to explain important financial concepts influencing investment markets today, without providing excruciating detail on their economic elements. You will learn what is truly driving our economy to better prepare you for our new economic future. It should help you identify long-term market trends, and is not a guide for day trading. My hope is you recognize the clear cause-and-effect relationship between the various forms of QE emanating from the US, and now embraced by most global central banks. It's an exciting topic, so let's get started!

CHAPTER 1

Confirming the
QE Effect on Stocks

*Those who cannot remember the past are
condemned to repeat it.*

George Santayana, poet and philosopher

The Federal Reserve System in the United States has been the single most powerful influence on the US stock market since the Great Recession of 2007 – 2009. Single-handedly, it drove stock prices higher in an attempt to avoid a new Great Depression and revive a struggling US economy. Yet when I speak to investors about this influence, few have a basic understanding of this important topic.

This book aims to change that.

Think about the opening statement for a moment, "The Federal Reserve has been the single most powerful influence in the US stock market since the Great Recession." The Fed, an organization which is not a US government agency, wields the greatest power to control US stocks. This power affects every 401(k) retirement plan, IRA, pension fund, endowment and foundation investment plan. More importantly, this affects YOU and your retirement. If you want to learn what really drives the stock market higher or lower, it is the Federal Reserve System. While it is true individual companies may buck the overall stock market trend if they launch a revolutionary product or service, it is the Federal Reserve that shapes our overall economic progress by controlling our financial system with its multi-trillion dollar balance sheet. Through its Quantitative Easing (QE) programs, it has firmly directed stock markets higher in the hope that elevated stock and asset prices will ultimately stimulate the broader economy.

"The Fed wields the greatest power to control US stocks."

Before discussing the Federal Reserve System (the Fed) and QE in detail, let's define QE and confirm its dominant control of the US stock market as measured by the movement in the S&P500 Stock Index. While the Fed has always played a role in helping to nudge stocks up or down with its policies (earning the prolific adage, *"Don't Fight the Fed"*), this cause-and-effect relationship has been most pronounced since QE1 was unleashed during the Great Recession in 2008.

Chart 1a shows the strong correlation between our addiction to QE and the corresponding response in the stock market. Once you recognize how striking this is, we will discuss the program in greater detail.

Chart 1a

S&P500 Index Chart (as of 10/13/16)

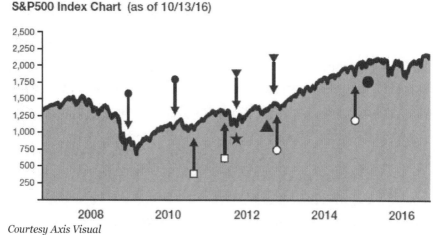

Courtesy Axis Visual

➤ QE1 and QE1+
☐➤ QE 2 (with Bernanke Hint)
▶➤ Operation Twist (with extension)
★ ECB Announces QE1
▲ Mario Draghi's "Whatever it Takes" comment
○➤ QE3 plus extensions
● ECB Implements QE1

A remarkable pattern emerges: A form of QE is announced; the stock market may hesitate while the news is digested, but eventually moves higher. As the QE program nears completion, the market looks for clues about the next round of stimulus. If none appear, stocks fall. A concerned Fed then turns on the stimulus spigot once again and the market moves higher until, you guessed it, the program ends and stocks falter.

"A form of QE is announced; the stock market may hesitate while the news is digested, but eventually moves higher."

Consequently, the market demands a greater degree of QE with each successive announcement in order to achieve the asset price inflation it seeks. It is literally that simple. Our economy and stock market have become addicted to QE.

And so far, we find it hard to end our addiction.

It's a Global Addiction

We will also discuss how it became a global addiction. Following the June 2016 Brexit vote, while the Fed remained on the sidelines, global central bankers jumped into action with the greatest monthly amount of QE foisted on global economies in history. This helped stabilize falling markets after the unexpected outcome of the vote.

Even the Bank of England (central bank of the United Kingdom) was forced to stabilize financial markets after Brexit. It lowered interest rates to a record low, pledged $130 billion of new funding to banks and bought $91 billion of government and corporate bonds. All with fabricated "money".

So, Just What Is QE?

In its simplest form, Quantitative Easing is action the Federal Reserve takes to stimulate a struggling economy. When the financial system is weak or in crisis, other primary sources of economic stimulus may be in decline (most notably the US consumer and corporations). As the "lender of last resort," the Fed is called upon to swap assets with banks and related financial institutions to improve their financial health.

"Quantitative Easing is action the Federal Reserve takes to stimulate a struggling economy."

QE is achieved in a variety of forms, whether the Fed exchanges low-quality and poor-performing investments held at banks with safer US Treasury securities, or makes four-week loans available to thousands of banks "to unclog the pipes of the credit system," in the words of former Treasury Secretary Timothy Geithner. During the Great Recession, when underperforming mortgage securities from Fannie Mae and Freddie Mac were causing distress for many banks, the Fed accepted these mortgage securities in exchange for US Treasury bonds to help instill financial confidence within banks and our economy.

Where does the Fed get the Treasury bonds in the first place? Well, they just appear. "Money" is fabricated out of thin air through the ability of the Fed to create Federal Reserve Notes, which are exchanged for other assets, typically fixed-income investments on deposit at banks and financial institutions. For an example of the latitude the Fed takes during times of financial stress, please read the comments below from former Fed Chairman Marriner Eccles during a 1941 congressional testimony and a description of the Fed's Commercial Paper Funding Facility (CPFF) employed in 2008.

1941 Congressional Testimony

It is difficult for Americans to comprehend that our total money supply is backed by nothing but debt. If everyone paid back all that was borrowed, there would be no money left in existence.

Allow this exchange between a former Fed Governor and a Congressman to help illustrate this point. Marriner Eccles was the Governor of the Fed in 1941. He was asked to give testimony before the House Committee on Banking and Currency on the role of the Fed leading up to the Great Depression. Congressman Wright Patman, Chairman of the Committee, asked how the Fed got the money to purchase two billion dollars' worth of government bonds in 1933.

Eccles: We created it.

Patman: Out of what?

Eccles: Out of the right to issue credit money.

Patman: And there is nothing behind it, is there, except our government's credit?

Eccles: That is what our money system is. If there were no debts in our money system, there wouldn't be any money.

Still confused? Perhaps this explanation will help. Robert Hemphill was the Credit Manager of the Federal Reserve Bank in Atlanta. In the foreword to a book by Irving Fisher, titled *100% Money*, Hemphill states:

> "If all bank loans were paid, no one could have a bank deposit, and there would not be a dollar of coin or currency in circulation. This is a staggering thought. We are

completely dependent on the commercial banks. Someone has to borrow every dollar we have in circulation, cash, or credit. If the banks create ample synthetic money we are prosperous; if not, we starve. We are absolutely without a permanent money system. When one gets a complete grasp of the picture, the tragic absurdity of our hopeless situation is almost incredible – but there it is."

With thanks for re-print permission from G. Edward Griffin, author of *The Creature from Jekyll Island*.

Federal Reserve's Commercial Paper Funding Facility (CPFF)

There were several causalities in the fall of 2008, as one financial calamity after another infected numerous institutions, some on the fringe of traditional financial firms (such as AIG insurance company and General Motors). As the lender of last resort, the Fed was called upon to finance many quasi-financial companies with heretofore unconventional methods (a testament to the historic severity of the Great Recession). One such unconventional response was the CPFF.

"The CPFF required the most expansive interpretation of Fed authority yet," explained former US Treasury Secretary Timothy Geithner in his well-written book, *Stress Test: Reflections on Financial Crises*. He continued, "The Fed can only lend against collateral, and the CPFF was designed for unsecured commercial paper, which by definition is not backed by collateral. It is just corporate IOUs."

Commercial paper (short-term loans issued by a corporation, with terms no longer than nine months, used to finance inventories and accounts receivable) is typically purchased by money market funds which came under pressure in 2008 when many funds faced record redemption requests. In order to enhance liquidity and contribute to the overall improvement of credit markets, the Federal Reserve Bank of New York (one of twelve Federal Reserve Banks across the country, part of the Federal Reserve System) purchased three-month paper and held it to maturity. Their action helped stabilize this segment of the financial markets, plugging one hole in a fragile dike of financial duress.

This action underscored the extraordinary pressure placed on the Federal Reserve System to address a deluge of financial anxieties arriving at their doorstep. It would take a creative Fed, using old and new methods, to bring (temporary?) financial stability to our economy.

For a synopsis of many Quantitative Easing programs, such as TAF, TSLF, PDCF, AMLF, TALF and Maiden Lane I, II, III, please refer to Appendix One.

Appendix One provides an expansive explanation of Fed reaction to events during the Great Recession.

It is important to remember that *consumer spending* is the primary component driving the growth of our economy. When consumers are reluctant or unable to continue a modest amount of spending, the economy will undoubtedly falter. Corporations, which prudently manage their financial resources, will generally be reluctant to spend during these times. Therefore, the Fed is called upon to fabricate assets to exchange with struggling banks and other financial institutions.

Many times the Fed will exchange US Treasury securities or Federal Reserve Notes for troubled assets, enabling financial institutions to immediately improve their stability. The Fed hopes that by providing this financial assurance, consumers and corporations develop confidence with the notion of borrowing money, thereby stimulating a faltering economy.

Author's note: The concept of "money printing" by the Federal Reserve is a complex and confusing concept to grasp. The same is true for the way the monetary system works in the US. The Fed actually creates bank reserves and uses these reserves to purchase debt instruments (think government or agency bonds) at one of its member banks. It's true that the Fed finances all of its activities through money creation, sometimes referred to as "*ex nihilo*" or "out of thin air." But the Fed primarily creates this money out of thin air within the Federal Reserve Bank System and does not technically insert this fabricated money into the traditional banking system. For sake of clarity, I adopt a less cumbersome explanation of the Fed's process throughout this book. For the purist who is keenly interested in the precise details of this process, please refer to Appendix Two. How money is created is likely quite different than what you believe. Fractional Reserve Banking, as taught in economic classes in years past, no longer exists.

With that, let's continue with a description of the Fed, one of the world's most powerful institutions, and the one likely to have the biggest financial impact on your investments.

OK, Now Define the Federal Reserve

The verb "obfuscate" comes to mind. Defined by *dictionary.com* as, "to make something obscure or unclear, especially by making it unnecessarily complicated." Hey, not bad! For a more traditional definition, try this:

> First of all, the Federal Reserve System in the United States is not a government entity. Fed governors, such as Janet Yellen, are private citizens and are not government employees. The Fed actually resembles a private corporation, but even that is not technically correct. It is subject to political control, yet it remains independent of political oversight. Perhaps the best way to describe the Federal Reserve System is to label it a cartel, defined by *dictionary.com* as "an alliance of business companies formed to control production, competition, and prices."

The Fed's organizational structure consists of three main components: the National Board of Governors, twelve Regional Reserve Banks and the Federal Open Market Committee. Its primary function is to control the nation's money supply by adjusting interest rates (through the Fed Funds Rate) and to alter the amount of liquidity within our economy (by creating money and subsequently buying securities, or reducing the amount of liquidity within the economy). The Fed was created to help finance banks during times of trouble and its unique ownership ensures banks and financial institutions remain a priority when decisions are made.

"The Fed was created to help finance banks during times of trouble and its unique ownership ensures banks and financial institutions remain a priority when decisions are made."

For a detailed description of the Fed, a truly opaque organiza-tion, skip to the dialog box on page 71 titled *Simply Stated: The Operating Structure of the Federal Reserve System.* Don't feel bewildered if you are still scratching your head after reading the narrative. Better yet, go to the Fed's own website and see if it does a better job of describing their form and structure: www.federal-reserve.gov. The website has a ".gov" domain name suffix, but it is not a US government agency. Obfuscation continues to this day!

The Fed's Important Dual Mandate

Let's continue by describing the primary goal of the Fed (besides acting as a large backstop for financial institutions in times of crisis.

The Federal Reserve in the US, otherwise known as a Central Bank, is tasked by Congress with the dual mandate of providing our economy with maximum employment and price stability. To do this, it employs a *Monetary Policy* consisting of several tools. The two most popular monetary policy tools are an adjustment in the Federal Funds Rate (increasing or decreasing interest rates) and the purchase of securities in the open market (to help stimulate confidence and lending).

While setting interest rates and purchasing securities are forms of QE, stocks are most significantly affected when the Fed buys or sells securities. Other methods the Fed can employ involve the manner in which it buys and sells US Treasuries (such as Operation Twist, explained further in this chapter) or the outright purchase of stocks in the US stock market. While debate remains if the Fed has commenced the purchase of stocks, it remains an option if other methods are not effective in achieving its dual mandate. For more on this theory, read about the Plunge Protection Team below.

The Plunge Protection Team

Ahhh ... the mythical Plunge Protection Team (PPT). I'm certain only a handful of high-ranking government officials and a few elite Wall Street insiders know the real truth about this operation. What we do know is that President Ronald Reagan assembled top advisors after the stock market crash of 1987 to learn what steps could be taken to cushion a sudden and sharp drop in stocks ("Black Monday" occurred on October 19, 1987 when the Dow dropped 508 points, or 22.6%, in a single day). Known as the Working Group on Financial Markets, this team implemented protocols to limit dramatic stock market drops from happening again. "Circuit breakers" were implemented to temporarily halt or suspend trading should a stock index experience a significant percentage drop in a single day.

Rumors suggest members of the Plunge Protection Team (a nickname first penned by the *Washington Post* in 1997) take steps to help ensure a healthy stock market, which generally moves in a positive direction. Members of this team are supposedly the secretary of the Treasury, the chairman of the Board of Governors of the Federal Reserve, the chairman of the SEC and the chairman of the Commodity Futures Trading Commission. Perhaps other high-level government officials and select Wall Street executives also provide guidance. One unconfirmed role of the PPT is to work with the Fed to purchase stocks or stock ETFs (Exchange Traded Funds) to stimulate the markets during times of weakness or duress. Whenever a large buyer enters the market with huge volume to reverse a sharp drop in stocks, the PPT is often rumored to be engaged.

This certainly is not an outlandish concept as the Japanese Central Bank openly admits to buying Japanese stock ETFs. According to Bloomberg, its buying has been so prolific, it actually owns more than half of the nation's market for exchange-traded stock funds. As for our Fed, many believe it has already purchased stocks or stock ETFs since the Great Recession, encouraging the market to continue its yearly rise. I place myself firmly in this camp as recent market evidence and Fed actions demonstrate its unwavering mandate to help prevent any prolonged downturn in stocks, no matter the cost.

So, should we expect the Fed to buy stocks in the next market panic? Or, has it already occurred and been kept secret by the Fed and Wall Street executives? I have a hunch the truth will reveal itself in the coming years.

How the Fed Stimulates the Economy by Lowering Rates

One of the primary methods the Fed uses to stimulate the economy is to lower the Fed Funds Rate. This is the interest rate at which banks lend excess reserves on deposit at the Fed to other banks overnight. In theory, if the Fed lowers this lending rate, it gives banks access to money with a low or no interest rate, allowing them to pass on the lower rate to their customers, who will be more inclined to borrow money and finance operations, such as a new project, buy back stock or expand their business. The opposite is also true, suggesting the Fed would raise rates if the economy is expanding too quickly and it wants to suppress growth.

"The Fed uses the Fed Funds Rate to either stimulate or suppress growth in the economy."

In September 2007, the Fed began its journey toward its Zero Interest Rate Policy (ZIRP) when it lowered the Fed Funds Rate from 5.25% to 4.75%, then gradually to zero by December 2008. It remained at zero until a long-promised hike in December 2015 occurred, pushing the rate off zero to 0.25%.*

Over the years, the Fed used the Fed Funds Rate as its primary weapon to achieve its mandates. Normally, the Fed will adjust this rate by a quarter of one percent in a predictable and telegraphed manner at the conclusion of a Federal Open Market Committee (FOMC) two-day meeting, which occurs eight times a year. During times of extreme concern in the economy, the Fed can hold emergency sessions and announce changes outside of these regularly scheduled meetings. It would not be unusual for it to move more than the customary 0.25% (such as the 0.50% reduction in the Fed Funds Rate on September 17, 2001, hours before the NYSE first opened after the 9/11 tragedy).

As we entered 2015, the Fed conditioned investors to expect a gradual increase in the Fed Funds Rate. Since QE3+ finally ceased at the end of October 2014, it was now time for the Fed to try and raise

---

* Author's note: Prior to this 0.25% rate hike, I was predicting the Fed would not raise rates in 2015 or 2016. However, I allowed for the small chance they would raise rates only once during this time because they had backed themselves into a corner and had to act, or risk losing credibility in the marketplace. I believe the Fed will regret the decision to raise rates in December 2015 and will return to ZIRP in the near future. The upcoming 2016 presidential election complicates matters, as a neutral Fed will be reluctant to fiddle with monetary policy unless the stock market and economic conditions compel it to act.

interest rates. Without the tailwind of QE3 and the prospect of a rate hike looming, the stock market was stuck in neutral during the first 7 months of the year as investors eagerly awaited any hint or news about a delay in rates or even a thought about QE4. It wasn't until the summer of 2015 when the Fed found the courage to try to raise rates.

This market serenity, confirmed by a stubbornly low VIX* reading over four months, was shattered in August 2015 as China reminded the Fed of its important role in global markets. As a warning to the Fed to keep rates at zero, the People's Bank of China (PBOC, China's Central Bank) authorized a modest devaluation of its currency, the yuan, in August. This sent the global markets in a tailspin, with the S&P500 Index falling from a high of 2103 on August 18, 2015, to a low of 1867, a drop of over eleven percent in six straight trading days. *Gulp.* Volatility skyrocketed, as measured by the VIX, climbing over 400% during this time - all because the PBOC wanted to warn the Fed not to raise interest rates at its September 17 FOMC meeting.

Astute market watchers were not surprised when the Fed kept rates at zero at the conclusion of its September 17 meeting. Citing concern about weak net exports and the need for continued progress toward maximum employment and price stability, the Fed went against Main Street expectations and signaled ZIRP was here to stay for a while longer. Investors initially cheered this news, sending the S&P500 to a three-week high, but the buying soon waned as global central banks remained quiet on their intentions to continue or expand their monetary policies.

---

* VIX: A popular measure of stock market volatility created by the Chicago Board Options Exchanges.

As markets fell, investors turned their attention to the all-important September jobs report from the Department of Labor (DOL) for more clues on the future of QE. Any relevant economic data point would be scrutinized, as only two FOMC meetings remained in 2015.

The DOL reported that only 142,000 jobs were created in September when 201,000 were expected. This jobs report offered something for everyone, a horrible labor report making stock market bears happy, albeit for a very short time (the S&P500 e-mini futures contracts were down 29 points after the announcement), to the bulls, with the S&P500 Index staging a remarkable one-day turnaround under the heading of "Bad News is Good News" once again. With knowledge that the Fed would keep interest rates at zero for the next few months, a confused stock market launched higher. You gotta love ZIRP! This time the advance was supported by global central banks, as they soon reaffirmed their support of easy money policies.

Once again this reaction proved that Fed policy truly drives the general direction of the stock market, reinforcing the adage that investors are warned "not to fight the Fed.

The Birth of QE1

While ZIRP can prod stocks to gently move higher, the purchase of fixed-income investments (such as US Treasury bonds or mortgage-backed securities) in the right amount can unleash a sustained and pronounced move. Modest amounts of asset swaps have been employed by the Fed for many years (a trickle each year to help the economy along, or larger sums prior to 1/1/2000 or immediately after 9/11/01). However, the Great Recession of 2007 – 2009 required the Fed to significantly escalate this program and the market demanded it continue virtually unabated until October 2014.

QE1 was launched in December 2008 when consumers were financially flat on their backs and corporations remained prudently cautious in an uncertain world. This left the Fed as the last viable entity to stimulate the economy. In the wake of several severe financial disruptions to Wall Street firms, most notably Bear Stearns, AIG and Lehman Brothers in 2008, the Fed came to the rescue of many firms that had grown too aggressive (a softer word than "greedy") with their trading activities.

Some Wall Street firms managing conservative money market mutual funds found a portion of their holdings were not as safe as they expected. Did they exceed the limits on internal compliance procedures? Perhaps. What we do know is these firms bought "safe" securities that were not safe anymore, and these purchases threatened their survival. As the financial panic in 2008 grew, several fund companies received an inordinate amount of redemption requests and were in danger of "breaking the buck."* The Fed couldn't sit idly by and allow a modern-day version of a "run on the bank" to bankrupt a company or money market fund. The Fed was created by bankers in the early 1900s to help rescue struggling financial institutions and this was its big chance to act.

Utilizing its ability to create money *ex nihilo* (out of thin air), the Fed decided to help money market mutual funds by purchasing under-valued assets at full market value with Federal Reserve Notes. Whew, another crisis averted, thanks to the Fed.

---

* One attractive feature of a money market mutual fund is a stable price, known as Net Asset Value. Money market mutual funds set this price at $1/ share and promise a modest rate of return to shareholders. For investors, this is their safe money and many were concerned during the Great Recession when it appeared a large fund would be forced to lower its price below $1.

But, there was more work to be done as other troubled firms raised their hands looking for help. Acting as a Wall Street Santa Claus, the Fed was busy in late 2008 announcing a host of fancy bailout programs, with acronyms, such as TAF, TSLF, PDCF, AMLF, CPFF, TALF, and Maiden Lane I, II, III (refer to Appendix One for a description of each). This was not the time to punish these venerable financial firms for their aggressive behavior. No, there would be plenty of time later to scold these firms and get their promise of structural change to ensure this catastrophe would not happen again ... right?

". . . the Fed decided to help money market mutual funds by purchasing under-valued assets at full market value with Federal Reserve Notes."

The first sustained Quantitative Easing effort – labeled QE1 – began November 25, 2008, when the Fed announced it would purchase $600 billion in mortgage-backed securities using fiat currency (see description below). With investor nerves beyond frayed and a serious market meltdown looming, investors viewed this initial attempt to steady markets as underwhelming and markets continued to crater. Anxious global markets were also looking to the US for stability, and they were not disappointed. On March 18, 2009, the Fed added an additional $750 billion purchase of mortgage-backed and Treasury securities, known as the extension of QE1 or simply QE1+. This was the elixir the markets were seeking, as they finally arrested their descent and found a stronger financial footing.

"Anxious global markets were also looking to the US for stability, and they were not disappointed."

Fiat Currency

Fiat currency is money deemed to be legal tender, based solely on the full faith and credit of the issuing government. Historically, most currencies were backed by a physical commodity, primarily gold or silver. If you wanted to exchange your paper bill for something more substantial, you would request an exchange for an equal amount of the underlying commodity.

As recently as 1964, the US Treasury issued $1 bills marked "Silver Certificate," enabling the holder to exchange the dollar bill for a silver dollar coin, until the practice stopped in 1968. Fiat money is based solely on faith, and derives from the Latin word for "it shall be." When President Nixon announced on August 15, 1971 that the US would no longer allow US currency to be converted into gold, this officially ended the US dollars' peg to gold and ushered in the ability of the Federal Reserve to create whatever amount of money it deemed prudent, without restraint.

With the S&P500 stock index falling more than fifty percent from its 2007 high, and several high-profile companies in serious distress (such as AIG, Merrill Lynch and Citigroup), it was no time to be timid. The US Treasury, knowing it could not rely solely on the Fed to stem the selling on Wall Street, simultaneously fought for and received approval from Congress to implement its own fiscal policy initiative, concurrent with QE1 (Chapter Three provides more detail). The positive effect from the combined fiscal policy from the US Treasury and Fed's monetary policy, however, was short-lived as the market continued downward soon after QE1+ ended in March 2010.

"The chart at the beginning of this chapter confirms the high correlation between Fed money creation and the move higher in the S&P500 stock index."

This prompted QE2. Originally proposed for serious consideration by Fed Chair Ben Bernanke at the annual retreat in Jackson Hole, Wyoming, for global central bankers in August 2010, this $600 billion program officially started in November 2010. But, the August hint alone was enough to send stocks decidedly higher until, you guessed it, the QE2 program ended in June 2011 and stocks began to fade. The chart at the beginning of this chapter confirms the high correlation between Fed money creation and the move higher in the S&P500 stock index.

What's Old Is New Again, with a Twist!

Once QE2 ended, it was apparent the economy was still too weak to stand on its own. The implementation of historic monetary and fiscal policy, and weak treasury receipts, began to take its toll on the stability of the US government, leading to the first ever down-grade in August 2011 of the US government's credit rating from AAA to AA+ by the Standard & Poor's rating agency. It was time for the Fed to act once again, but concern mounted in Washington political circles that the Fed was becoming far too aggressive with the expansion of its balance sheet at the risk of inducing high inflation. Stealing an idea from the Fed's playbook in 1961, it was time for the Fed to try something different ... with a "Twist."

First employed in 1961 by the Fed to stimulate the economy, Operation Twist was utilized once again in September 2011 to sell short-term US fixed-income securities with maturities of less than three years, in exchange for the same amount of longer-term bonds between six and thirty years. The initial Operation Twist, targeting $400 billion in bond swaps, was originally slated to end in June 2012, but was extended with an additional $267 billion in bond swaps from July 2012 through December 2012, in response to sluggish US growth.

If the Fed is concerned about increasing its balance sheet, but still needs to combat a weak economy, it can employ this technique as it does not require creation of any money. By purchasing longer-term Treasuries, it seeks to reduce interest rates with the hope of stimulating lending.

As the Fed continued to dole out its financial support, it became obvious the markets were addicted to QE programs, as the pattern went like this: The Fed initiates stimulus to stem weakness in asset prices, waits to see if the economy can stand on its own two feet, finds it cannot, implements even more stimulus, hopes this time it will be enough, finds it is not and stimulates once again. The pattern continues to this day, and is expected to continue for a very long time.

QE ... Until the Fed Says Stop!

Up to this point, the Fed deliberately announced the amount of stimulus it was adding to the economy and the expected end date. Knowing this, investors were anxious in the weeks lead-ing up to the end of a program, waiting for news of the next QE effort and gauging its expected impact on the economy. Sensing this, Fed official decided to act well before the end of Operation Twist and announced QE3 in September 2012. As if that wasn't enough, it also declared this QE program to be open-ended, earning the nickname "QE-Infinity."

One would think the stock market would have embraced this news and send stocks decidedly higher. Unfortunately, this was not the case. With economic conditions still below levels deemed satisfactory by the Fed, the stock market fell almost 9% in the following weeks. Knowing this was not the time to be timid again, the Bernanke Fed announced in December 2012 that it would more than *double* the money creation, from $40 billion a month to $85 billion a month ... and would con-tinue until it decided to stop. Now that's more like it! The Fed was finally getting the message: Investors wanted a higher amount of QE with each new announcement, and they wanted it to continue for a longer period of time.

"The Fed was finally getting the message: Investors wanted a higher amount of QE with each new announcement, and they wanted it to continue for a longer period of time."

Boom! This unleashed the type of asset price inflation the Fed was seeking, sending the S&P500 stock index up over 31% in the next twelve months. Yay Fed! With inflation in check and stocks moving higher, talk of an out-of-control Fed diminished as a rising stock market cures many ills.

However, even a great party has to end sometime, and QE3-Infinity was no exception. Sensing an elevated stock market can finally allow the Fed to ease back on the QE throttle, it telegraphed a slow and steady reduction in asset purchases and money creation beginning February 2014 and ending in October 2014.

Judging by the first nine months of 2014, this strategy appeared to be working. Stocks continued their climb (because the Fed was still buying bonds, albeit at a reduced rate), rising 10% from January 2014 to mid-September 2014. Could it be this easy to unwind QE?

Unfortunately, no.

With investors getting nervous that their QE addiction would finally end in October, they headed for the exits in a hurry. In just three weeks, from September 19 to October 15, 2014, the stock market lost 9.8%, erasing all of the year-to-date gains in less than a month. "Where's my next QE?" they seemed to demand.

With the Fed sensing a panic in stocks surging once again, it was time to reassure investors it knew what it was doing. First, it trotted out St. Louis Fed Governor James Bullard on October 15, a day when the Dow Jones Industrial Average was down 461 points, with a message indicating QE4 **could** be announced if conditions warranted. Boom! Another crisis averted with the promise of more QE. The Dow rebounded almost 300 points on the news, ending the day down just 174 points. Simply amazing. The market was responding to QE like one of Pavlov's dogs.

But wait, the Fed wanted to make sure this was a sustainable rally. QE had become a global addiction and the Fed wanted to ensure other central banks were doing their part. Accordingly, the Fed was pleased when the European Central Bank (ECB), Bank of Japan (BOJ, the central bank of Japan) and the Peoples Bank of China each announced their own form of QE, just in time to ensure a Santa Claus stock market rally into year's end. In fact, the dramatic move from the October 15 lows through December 5th marked one of the strongest and sustained short-term rallies on Wall Street, ever. Not only was QE back, but it had gone global! Behind closed doors, the Fed was certainly all smiles from the results of its global coordination of QE.

"Not only was QE back, but it had gone global!"

But the sugar high of global QE didn't last long enough to satisfy investors through 2015. The US stock market drifted between gains and losses most of the year, as the world's central banks sporadically parsed out news pertaining to their own attempts to stimulate their respective economies. As you will read later, China plays a significant role in efforts to stem a sharp drop in its stock market, economy and GDP.

Recap of QE Asset Purchases

Let's pause and summarize the effect QE asset purchases had on the US stock market from 2008 through 2015. It entailed a heroic effort by the Fed as it created almost $4 trillion with the touch of a keystroke, clearly a record in its 102-year history. As a visual reminder, Chart 1b describes what the Fed attempts to accomplish with QE:

Chart 1b

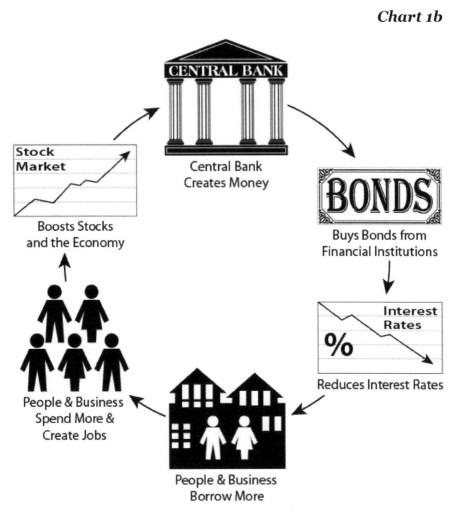

CENTRAL BANK

Central Bank
Creates Money

BONDS

Buys Bonds from
Financial Institutions

Stock
Market

Boosts Stocks
and the Economy

Interest
Rates
%

Reduces Interest Rates

People & Business
Spend More &
Create Jobs

People & Business
Borrow More

Courtesy Peregrine Associates

So, Just How Much Is a Trillion?

So far, we have described the creation of trillions of dollars to rescue a weak economy. Yet, we throw around the $1 trillion figure with ease. But, how much is $1 trillion? Literally, $1 trillion is a one followed by twelve zeros: $1,000,000,000,000. OK, that's a big number, but it's still hard for many people to comprehend. To better understand just how prolific the Fed's actions have been - increasing its balance sheet from $900 billion in 2008 to $4.5 trillion today - let's wrap our arms around $1 trillion. Figuratively, of course!

- If you earned $34 million dollars *every day,* you would wait more than 80 *years* to have $1 trillion (and to think, the Fed created over $1 trillion in 2008 in just a matter of *months*!).

- If you laid $1 bills end-to-end, one trillion $1 bills would stretch from the earth to the moon ... *406 times.*

- If you were flying a supersonic jet at *the speed of sound* unfurling a roll of one trillion $1 bills, you would have to fly the jet non-stop for 14.4 **years** in order to release $1 trillion.

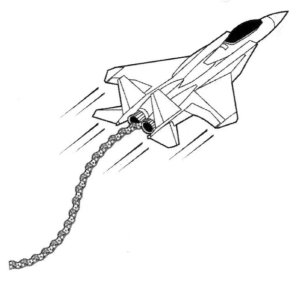

Graphic credit: Tigerblaez @ Fiverr.com

Whenever I read these examples, it never ceases to amaze me of the magnitude of $1 trillion. And the examples refer to *just* $1 trillion. Not only has the Fed created almost $4 trillion in the past eight years, the US government debt has ballooned to almost $20 trillion. Yikes, I'll ignore that topic for another time. Double gulp.

Chapter 1 Summary

Since QE3+ ended in October 2014, the only stimulus the Fed exerts on the markets is keeping rates near zero. Therefore, stock markets currently remain stagnant ... clinging to the belief that the Fed will orchestrate more QE from its global central bank partners (since it is too soon for the Fed to ride to the rescue with QE4). If more global QE is not forthcoming, stocks will signal their dismay with heightened volatility and a significant decline, demanding the Fed respond with the QE4 fix markets expect.

Make no mistake, QE4 will be upon us in the near future. The amount of turmoil the markets will endure in order to get the announcement remains to be seen. Stock markets are clearly addicted to QE and it will be very difficult to wean us off this addiction.

Now that we have confirmed QE is responsible for driving stock prices higher, it's time to turn our attention to how we got into this mess in the first place.

- There is a remarkable correlation between the implementation of QE, both domestic and global, that drives the US stock market higher when announced, and weakens and falls when the program ends.
- Quantitative Easing is defined as measures the Fed takes to stimulate a faltering economy. Most notably, purchasing

fixed-income investments from financial institutions in exchange for money the Fed fabricates from thin air.

- The Federal Reserve is not a government agency, it is not Federal and it does not have any Reserves. Its form and structure is complicated, allowing a quasi-private organization the ability to create any amount of US currency it deems prudent, without permission from the Federal government, in secret meetings - the only group on the planet with the power to do so.

- QE1 & QE1+ announced November 2008 and ended March 2010, adding $1.4 trillion.

- QE2 announced August 2010 and ended June 2011, adding $600 billion.

- Operation Twist announced September 2011 and ended December 2012. It did not add to the Fed's balance sheet, but it exchanged short-dated Treasuries for longer-dated Treasuries.

- QE3 and QE3+ announced September 2012 and ended October 2014, adding $1.7 trillion.

- The Fed Funds Rate remained near zero from December 2008 until a token 0.25% increase was announced in December 2015.

- Numerous forms of QE were announced by Central Bank partners around the globe, most notably from Europe (the ECB), Japan and China.

- Total amount of money electronically created by the Fed in just six years, $3.6 trillion (over 1,500 dollar-bill trips to the moon or flying non-stop at supersonic speed for over 53 years).

CHAPTER **2**

How Did We Get into This Mess?

The mind that opens to a new idea never comes back to its original size.

Albert Einstein

To prevent the economy from sliding into the abyss of a new Depression, the Federal Reserve and US Treasury employed extreme and unprecedented measures during the Great Recession of 2007 – 2009. This chapter discusses the circumstances that allowed the economy to get into this fragile condition. Specifically:

· Once the US left the gold standard in 1971, the US Treasury and Fed could increase our monetary reserves with few restrictions.

· The result was a dramatic increase in our Total Credit Market Debt, from $1 trillion in the 1960s to over $65 trillion today.

· US consumers' penchant for buying "stuff" allowed the US Current Account Balance to explode, fueling global economies. This was one of the most important economic developments in the 20th century.

· The US consumer drives two-thirds of our GDP growth. Several indicators suggest the ability to continue their spending is weak.

- When consumer spending finally declined in 2007, the economy contracted in dramatic fashion, forcing the Fed to support weak financial institutions as "the lender of last resort."

- Furthermore, the Fed stimulated the economy (asset prices) with a Zero Interest Rate Policy (ZIRP).

- As you read the facts and study the charts, you'll notice many of these significant economic events haven't occurred in decades. Some have never occurred in the history of our great country. This underscores the severity of current economic conditions.

It is important to remember that US consumers account for about two-thirds of our GDP output. Approaching 2008, consumers had literally tapped out their credit cards and home equity credit lines. Corporations, the second of three primary drivers of our GDP, had money to spend, but remained prudent stewards of their financial resources. After all, they couldn't afford to be financially reckless like consumers, as they had to answer to a board of directors or others to ensure the stability of the company during turbulent times.

GDP is the total market value of all final goods and services produced in a country in a year.

This left the Fed and US Treasury as the last entities able to stop the economic freefall and restore confidence. The US Treasury could employ certain tactics, but it is much harder for them to act on a moment's notice (Chapter Three explains why in greater detail). However, the Fed was specifically created to address such a panic.

To understand why the US consumer commanded such a dominant role in the expansion of our GDP, let's begin with a brief history of gold, culminating with important decisions made in 1968 and 1971. These decisions authorized fiat money and unleashed an historic rise in the creation of credit (fiat money is currency not backed by gold or a similar commodity).

The Gold Standard

Under the gold standard, the amount of money a country could keep in circulation was relatively finite, allowing for a modest increase each year as more gold was mined and distributed around the world. A nation printed paper currency and backed the currency with a precious metal, such as gold, to give consumers a high degree of comfort that their currency was backed by a tangible asset.

In theory, a country would keep physical gold in storage representing a portion of the amount of currency they printed. More gold discoveries, or increases of gold due to trade, would allow the government to print more money. Paper currency could be exchanged for gold, but it was much easier to carry paper currencies and transact business with paper notes than gold coins or bars. Gold has been used to back currency since 643 BC in Lydia (present-day Turkey).

Trade between countries had to balance, more or less, and the convertibility of paper currency into gold was a method of keeping trade between countries in check. This practice became commonplace in the mid-1800s as trade between countries flourished due to advances in transportation. Most of the dominant countries participating in an emerging global economy adopted the gold standard to facilitate trade. Below is an example of how the gold standard helped maintain economic balance.

Currency Use under a Gold Standard

If a country, perhaps England, would buy an excessive amount of goods from France, the French would be paid in English currency, which could be converted into gold. However, the amount of gold England held was finite, and as its imports grew (sending English currency and physical gold to France), its ability to buy items decreased (it was exchanging English gold for French goods). As its ability to buy items decreased, the English economy would slow down or fall into recession as unemployment rose, wages stagnated and deflation caused prices to fall.

The French, on the other hand, would do quite well. It would enjoy the benefits of selling its items to the English. Yet, over the years, inflation would creep into its economy. The French, finding items in England more affordable due to falling prices, would subsequently increase its purchase of English goods. The pendulum would shift, as more French currency returned to England and equilibrium in trade was restored. These economic cycles were commonplace and not viewed as times of panic when the trade difference was unbalanced.

Adherence to the gold standard allowed global trade to comfortably ebb and flow until WWI. As war broke out in 1914, European countries found it necessary to abandon their currencies' convertibility into gold so they could print more money to purchase war materials.

Chart 2a

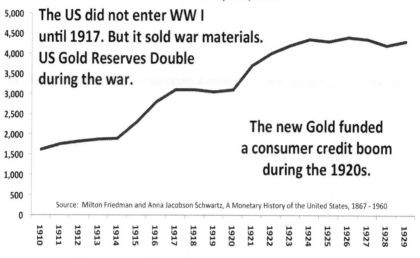

US Gold
1910 to 1929, US$ mn

The US did not enter WW I until 1917. But it sold war materials. US Gold Reserves Double during the war.

The new Gold funded a consumer credit boom during the 1920s.

Source: Milton Friedman and Anna Jacobson Schwartz, A Monetary History of the United States, 1867 - 1960

━━Gold component of high-powered money inside and outside the Treasure US$ mn

Courtesy Richard Duncan Economics

The US stayed out of WWI until 1917, enabling the US to supply both sides of the war with desperately needed materials, often paid for with dwindling gold reserves (since most countries devalued their currency by excessive money printing, gold was a preferred medium of exchange). This enabled the US to significantly increase its gold reserves and led to prosperous times, known as the Roaring Twenties. For a fascinating look at the adverse effect of excessive money printing in the early 1920s, see below.

The Weimar Republic

To illustrate how quickly a country can destroy its economy with excessive money printing, we'll turn to Germany in the early 1920s.

The Weimar Republic marked the time in Germany after WWI when hyperinflation crippled its economy. At the conclusion of the war, the German government was in disarray owing to frequent changes in political leadership. Compounding the matter was mounting financial pressure on a weak and fledgling government. Unable to say no to those demanding financial payments, the German government responded by printing an ever-increasing amount of its currency, the Deutsche Mark.

In 1914, just before WWI broke out, a German mark was worth about 24 US cents (4.2 marks would buy one US dollar). By 1920, it would take 65 marks to buy a single US dollar, making a mark worth about 1.5 cents. At this time, financial demands on the German government were many, both from within and outside the country. In addition to paying for its own war expenses, there were pension payments to war veterans, disbursements to those who lost property and expanded social programs for those who lost jobs or needed health care. Adding to the mounting internal pressure was the demand by victorious countries for war reparations. Since the mark was no longer tied to a gold standard, the easy answer was to print more marks. A lot more. Literally tons more.

The speed in which it printed money is hard to fathom. In 1922, about $1 trillion marks of additional currency was printed. In the first *six months* of 1923, it exploded to $17 trillion marks. Today, computers make it easy to electronically print a trillion dollars. In 1923, it took 133 printing facilities with 1,783 machines and more than 30 paper mills to meet the escalating demand for paper marks.

The result? By August 1923, a US dollar bought 620,000 marks (remember, in 1914, one dollar would buy only four marks). Just three months later, one dollar bought 630 billion marks. That's right, 630 *billion*, when three months earlier Germans were counting in thousands. A slab of butter cost 250 billion marks. A ride on a Berlin street car, which had cost one mark before the war, was now 15 billion. In the time it took someone to drink a cup of coffee in a café, the price was likely to double. People were known to haul their money around in duffel bags or wheelbarrows. The story is told of a citizen reporting the theft of his wheelbarrow full of money to police, because he was more concerned about the return of his wheelbarrow than the money inside.

Not only is this lesson of hyperinflation etched in the memories of many German politicians and financiers, it stands as a warning from those who support a gold standard. However, with the present-day structure of global central banks, there is little chance a developed economy will return to a gold standard in our lifetime.

Unfortunately, all good things must come to an end and the late 1920s signaled the beginning of very harsh times in the US. As credit dried up in 1930, the world was thrust into a global depression due to an excessive credit bubble that ruptured. Countries attempting to return to a gold standard quickly reversed course. As the price of gold rose in the US, people redeemed dollars for gold, seriously depleting gold reserves. The Federal Reserve tried to increase the value of the dollar by raising interest rates, but this just hastened the oncoming depression. In 1933, newly elected

President Franklin D. Roosevelt halted the convertibility of gold and ordered Americans to turn in their gold for US dollars. Ineffective and uncoordinated action by the US government and Federal Reserve allowed the Depression to drag on until WWII, when our economy was stimulated as Americans supplied war materials and worked with our allies to win the war.

To complete this brief history of gold in America, the 1944 Bretton Woods Agreement once again established the gold standard at a fixed price of $35 per ounce. Since the US held most of the world's gold, many countries recognized the US dollar as the world's official reserve currency and pegged the value of their currency to the dollar.

The Bretton Woods Agreement of 1944

In July 1944, an historic financial conference took place in Bretton Woods, New Hampshire, which included 730 delegates from all 44 Allied nations. The primary purpose was to help establish financial order after the expected conclusion of WWII.

Primary outcomes included the establishment of the World Bank, the International Monetary Fund and formal acknowledgment of the US dollar as the world's reserve currency. By doing so, Bretton Woods established a fixed exchange rate for the US dollar and gold at $35 per ounce. This essentially placed the majority of the world's currencies on a pseudo gold standard as well, since each member agreed to redeem its currency for dollars, not gold. At that time, the US held about three-fourths of the world's supply of gold and was the emerging leader of the world.

The economic boom that followed the end of WWII boosted international trade and supported the export of US dollars overseas. Due to the Marshall Plan, private sector investment and US military spending overseas, foreign countries amassed a growing amount of US currency, which was still convertible into gold. Fearing inflation and the shrinking real value of the US dollar, foreign governments increased their conversion of dollars for gold. This deeply concerned politicians in Washington as a steady stream of gold flowed out of Ft. Knox to destinations overseas.

Chart 2b

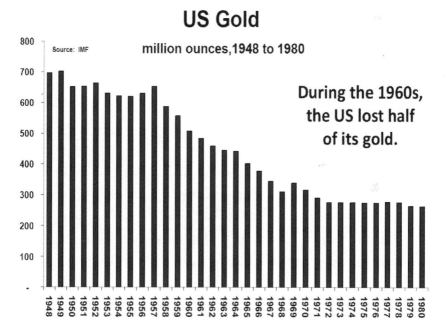

US Gold

million ounces,1948 to 1980

Source: IMF

During the 1960s, the US lost half of its gold.

Courtesy Richard Duncan Economics

It wasn't until the 1960s when the gold standard finally broke down, culminating in the August 15, 1971 announcement on national TV by President Richard Nixon that the US would no longer back the dollar with gold. The timing of the announcement was so important, the president interrupted the most popular TV show in America, *Bonanza*, on a Sunday evening before the markets opened the next day.

This action finally removed gold as an impediment, allowing the US to create whatever amount of money it deemed prudent. Today, with the US government national debt and Federal Reserve obligations rising into the many trillions of dollars, there is little hope of the US ever returning to the gold standard.

Let the Buying Begin!

The US government has a propensity to let programs it creates get out of hand (shocking, no doubt!). Take the IRS for example. In 1913, the 16th Amendment gave Congress the authority to enact an income tax. On the first Form 1040, Congress authorized a 1% tax on net personal incomes above $3,000 and a 6% surtax on income of more than $500,000. Only five years later, as the US was fully immersed in WWI, the top income tax rate rose to 77%. After the War, it fell to 24% in 1929 and rose again during the Depression. While the first income tax initially targeted the upper-middle class and above ($3,000 in 1913, inflation adjusted, is over $73,000 in 2016), it was easy for politicians to tweak rates and regulations in order to achieve their desired revenue goals.

The point being, once the IRS was established, it was much easier for subsequent politicians to make adjustments to this program to meet their needs. The same is true for the Federal Reserve System. Once the Federal Reserve Act created the Fed, subsequent Fed governors felt free to modify the amount of currency in our economy to meet their needs. The big difference however, is that Congress must authorize any increase or decrease in tax rates. Not so for the Fed, since it is a private agency and is no longer tied to a gold standard. It can simply create whatever amount of US currency it deems prudent without any authorization from the government. Now that is ultimate power.

This unparalleled combination of our ability to create money, and our status as the world's reserve currency, allowed US consumers to assume a record amount of credit/debt. How much credit? An historic amount, over $65 trillion since the 1960s.

Chart 2c

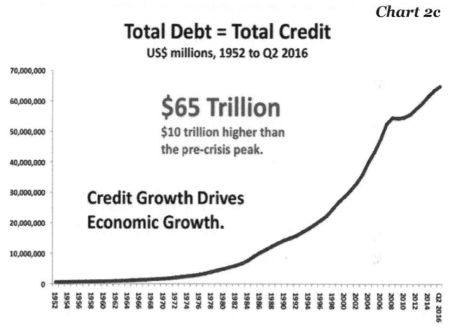

Total Debt = Total Credit
US$ millions, 1952 to Q2 2016

$65 Trillion

$10 trillion higher than the pre-crisis peak.

Credit Growth Drives Economic Growth.

Source: Fed, Financial Accounts of the United States

Courtesy of Richard Duncan Economics

Credit growth drives economic growth, and when the US stopped backing dollars with gold in 1968 and 1971, credit exploded. Rising from $1 trillion in the 1960s, Chart 2c shows total credit market debt growing virtually unabated through six recessions until the Great Recession in 2008, only to resume its climb to over $65 trillion today. Even the stock market correction of 2000 – 2003 couldn't slow this prolific spending trend.

In tandem with the growth of credit and popularity of credit cards, the US housing boom ignited in the 1990s and continued unabated until the abrupt disruption in 2007. Combining a reduction in interest rates with the proliferation of home mortgage companies (aided by a federal mandate for Fannie Mae and Freddie Mac to support an easy mortgage policy), homeowners could refinance their homes at lower interest rates *and* withdraw equity from their home, while keeping mortgage payments the same. Therefore, rising home prices and falling interest rates allowed the homeowner to fund an addition, a pool or new kitchen without increasing their monthly mortgage payment. What a country! This new-found source of credit allowed the US consumer, who is responsible for about two-thirds of our GDP growth each year, to stimulate domestic and global economies in a dramatic fashion.

The growth of consumer credit spending led to an increasing imbalance in trade between the US and its trading partners, such as China, Japan and the European Union. This proliferation of credit led to another important economic development of the 20th century ... the US Current Account Balance.

The Importance of the US Current Account Balance

Many readers likely remember the excessive inflation our country experienced after we left the gold standard in 1971. Peaking in the early 1980s, an astute investor could have purchased 30-year US government bonds paying over 14.5%. Imagine having the US government paying a 14.5% return on your investment every year from 1981 to 2011. Nice, indeed.

However, back in 1981, inflation was equally high, with mortgage rates over 18% as an example, making the real return on a 14.5% government bond a questionable investment if high inflation were to persist.

But it didn't, thanks to one of the most important economic developments in the 20th century, an exploding US current account balance (Chart 2d).

Because of globalization, US consumers were able to benefit from billions of very poor people willing to work for a few dollars a day. Cheap labor prices, most notably from China, pushed down the price of "stuff" in America and helped tame high inflation. With our new-found ability to buy on credit (such as credit cards fueling credit growth and the US no longer tied to the gold standard), our total credit exploded (remember Chart 2c), allowing our economy to prosper.

The US stock market also flourished as companies sold more products and profits soared. As a result, the S&P500 index climbed from 200 in 1985 to 1,500 in 2000. To put this in perspective, it took the S&P500 index over 17 years to double, from 100 in 1968 to 200 in 1985. Because of our explosive buying binge, the S&P rose over six-fold in less than 15 years, from November 1985 to March 2000. You will soon learn that robust US consumer spending powered us though the stock market set-back in the early 2000s, only to finally tire in 2007, leading to the Great Recession. It was then that the Federal Reserve took up the spending slack with its QE programs to power the stock market higher.

Chart 2d shows the result of this imbalance in consumer spending as US consumers fueled the growth of economies around the globe.

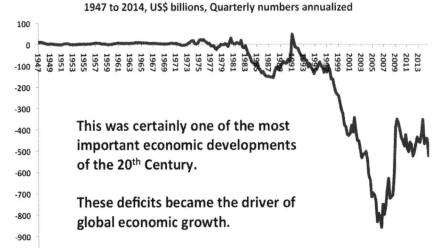

US Current Account Balance
1947 to 2014, US$ billions, Quarterly numbers annualized

This was certainly one of the most important economic developments of the 20th Century.

These deficits became the driver of global economic growth.

Source: St Louis Fed

Courtesy of Richard Duncan Economics

The Current Account Balance is an important indicator of economic health, and primarily reflects the difference between a nation's net imports and exports (think trade deficit or trade surplus). A positive current account balance (trade surplus) indicates a nation is a net lender to the rest of the world, while a negative current account balance (trade deficit) indicates it is a net borrower from the rest of the world.

> *"A positive current account balance indicates a nation is a net lender to the rest of the world, while a negative current account balance indicates it is a net borrower from the rest of the world."*

As you surmised from Chart 2d, the US holds the world's largest trade deficit, by a wide margin - more than twice the deficit of #2 United Kingdom.

This chart is important as it verifies the effect net imports had on our trade deficit as a result of US consumers buying more stuff on credit. The more we buy, the more we import, increasing our trade deficit. This imbalance allowed our overseas trading partners to thrive, and subsequently, their trading partners to prosper as well. However, when we slow our spending, the economies of our trade partners contract, causing a domino effect to their suppliers. As the world's number one GDP leader, a robust US consumer and economy is vital to global growth and stability. This is yet another reason the Fed remains constantly engaged with our economy and central banks around the world, to help manufacture steady global growth.

As we move toward an examination of how significant the Fed's action was in 2008 to prevent the Great Recession from becoming the next Depression, let's continue with a discussion on the financial health of the US consumer during the past seven years. It is my belief the typical US consumer is still financially challenged for a variety of reasons. If true, then we must continue to rely on the Federal Reserve to stoke the flames of economic growth whenever the economy falters. This means more money creation and zero interest rate policies (ZIRP) with the Fed finding some reason to reverse the 0.25% increase in the Fed Funds Rate it mistakenly raised in December 2015. Furthermore, as our economy suffers from the lack of stimulus, the Fed will be forced to announce QE4.

Let's begin with a discussion on wages and stagnating real wage growth. As Chart 2e depicts, inflation-adjusted pay of the typical US consumer has not increased much over the past 25 years. This means most Americans still have the same purchasing power they had in the late 1980s. It's no wonder many households remain in debt, as they find credit an easy way to buy more without having money to pay for it at the time of purchase.

Chart 2e

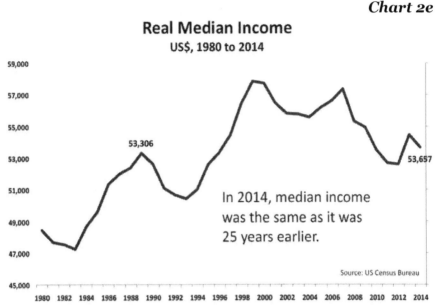

Real Median Income
US$, 1980 to 2014

In 2014, median income was the same as it was 25 years earlier.

Source: US Census Bureau

Courtesy Richard Duncan Economics

Corporations are "prudent stewards of their financial resources"

While consumers remain the primary driver of our GDP growth, corporations are number two on the list. If shoppers curtail their spending habits, it may be up to corporations to pick up the spending slack. Are they inclined to do so? With a very weak start to 2016, the Reuters news agency may provide a clue from a February 2016 article:

> Fearing lean times, U.S. companies tighten purse strings

> "The capital spending slump that originated in the hard-hit energy sector appears to be spreading more widely across other U.S. industries. Companies cutting or flat-lining their

capital expenditures in 2016 outpace those that say they will increase spending **by a factor of more than two to one**, according to a Reuters analysis. Companies in industries as diverse - and relatively strong - as healthcare, consumer goods and restaurants are among those tightening their belts in yet another sign that economic growth in 2016 may be anemic."

If this is an indication that consumers and corporations are curtailing their spending ways, all eyes will turn to the Fed and global central bankers for decisive action in the form of more QE. And make no mistake, it will come.

How About That Unemployment Rate!

One of the most celebrated victories the Fed claims from its QE efforts is a reduction in the unemployment rate. As a reminder, Congress charged the Fed with a "dual mandate" to maximize employment and provide price stability. Therefore, it is a remarkable achievement that the Fed reports unemployment falling from 10% during the Great Recession to 5% today. Great job! But we hear about "discouraged workers" and a low "Labor Force Participation Rate." How do they factor into the unemployment rate? Is today's unemployment rate really accurate?

First, the Bureau of Labor Statistics states:

Discouraged workers are defined as a subset of persons marginally attached to the labor force. The marginally attached are those persons not in the labor force who want and are available for work, and who have looked for a job sometime in the prior 12 months, but were not counted as unemployed because they had not searched for work in the four weeks preceding the survey. Among the marginally attached, discouraged workers were not currently looking for work specifically because they believed no jobs were available for them or there were none for which they would qualify.

OK, so it appears these are people who want to work and have looked for work, but since they found no work they are no longer looking for work. Yeah, I would be discouraged too. However, these discouraged workers are *not* counted in the unemployment statistics, even though they are *not employed*, are able-bodied and *want to work*. Funny math, if you ask me.

Another topic of interest regarding the health of the US consumer is the Labor Force Participation Rate.

Chart 2f

US. Bureau of Labor Statistics, Civilian Labor Force Participation Rate, retrieved from FRED, Federal Reserve Bank of St. Louis https://research.stlouisfed.org/fred2/series/, May 4, 2016.

Who Is FRED?

Throughout this book I refer to charts from "FRED." The FRED charts come directly from an extremely useful public website operated by the Federal Reserve Bank of St. Louis. It regularly updates thousands of charts to promote economic education and enhance economic research. Its research, charts and statistics are vital to a large contingent of economists, financial professionals and those of us interested in our economy. For more on FRED, visit https://research.stlouisfed.org.

The Labor Force Participation Rate is defined as the percentage of citizens who are employed, or unemployed but looking for a job. Got it? Yes ... this is a measure of people who are employed, and also counts people who are *not employed*, but looking for a job. Why? Perhaps to make the numbers look better (more funny math here?).

Chart 2f shows employment participation has actually been declining since the 2001 recession, and it continues to put a drag on the US consumer's ability to spend. Furthermore, at a current rate near 63%, it has fallen to levels last seen in the late 1970s. Typically, the more people work, the more income they have and the more they spend. And, as we explained, their ability to spend is vitally important to our national and international economies. With Americans facing stagnating real income and a falling labor force participation rate, it is no wonder many citizens are reluctant to spend.

"With Americans facing stagnating real income and a falling labor force participation rate, it is no wonder many citizens are reluctant to spend."

A Final Chart on Employment

QE had the effect of increasing full-time employment back to pre-Great Recession levels, one of the Fed's mandates. At what cost? The economy added about 10 million workers lost during the Great Recession at a cost of over $4 trillion in Fed and government stimulus. If the economy falters due to a lack of continued Fed stimulus, it is likely layoffs will ensue, generating expectations of further action by the Fed.

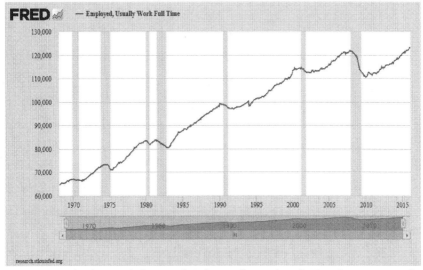

US. Bureau of Labor Statistics, Employed, Usually Work Full Time [LNS12500000], retrieved from FRED, Federal Reserve Bank of St. Louis https://research.stlouisfed.org/fred2/series/LNS12500000, May 4, 2016.

To bring us full circle, a final credit boom fueled by an over-heated housing market lead consumers to the doorstep of 2007, when our credit bubble burst and plunged the economy into the Great Recession. This was the tipping point as consumers were already weakened by stagnant real wage growth and tepid employment numbers. With the economy imploding, the Fed rode to the rescue with an eager checkbook.

Mid-Chapter Summary

Once we abandoned the gold standard, the Fed could create any amount of currency it deemed prudent. With the Fed encouraging a modest expansion of monetary supply over the decades, it armed the US consumer with the ability to go into debt to support a trade imbalance. When consumers finally couldn't absorb any more debt, the lack of spending tipped the US economy into the Great Recession. The Fed, as spender of last resort, then stepped in to bail out financial institutions that were feeling the painful withdrawal of the lack of consumer spending.

Expansion of the Fed's Balance Sheet

We now arrive at this book's seminal theory, that Quantitative Easing is largely responsible for the dramatic increase in asset prices since the Great Recession.

It is best to illustrate the Fed's historic spending with two charts, beginning with the following iconic chart showing the Fed's total money creation since 2003. Remember the shape of this line, as it will be referenced throughout the book.

Once the Great Recession hit, Fed spending exploded, sending $1.4 trillion dollars to numerous financial institutions within a matter of months and creating a total of $3.6 trillion in six years. Total assets on this chart rose from $900 billion in 2008 to $4.5 trillion today.

Chart 2g

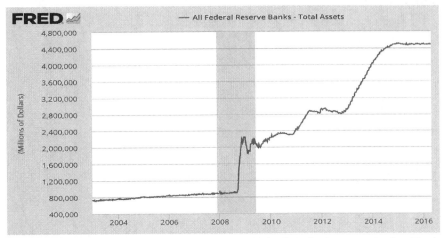

Board of Governors of the Federal Reserve System (US), All Federal Reserve Banks - Total Assets [WALCL], retrieved from FRED, Federal Reserve Bank of St. Louis https://research. stlouisfed.org/fred2/series/WALCL, May 4, 2016.

Notice how the Fed typically engineered a modest and steady expansion of its creation each year from 2003 – 2008.

How does this compare to past bouts of crisis spending? Chart 2h clearly illustrates the massive amount of money the Fed added to the US economy in response to the Great Recession.

Chart 2h

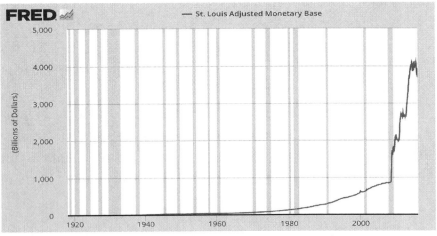

Federal Reserve Bank of St. Louis, St. Louis Adjusted Monetary Base [AMBSL], retrieved from FRED, Federal Reserve Bank of St. Louis https://research.stlouisfed.org/fred2/series/AMBSL, May 4, 2016.

- **1929 – 1939**: The Fed was largely confused and ineffective in its response to the Great Depression, providing modest monetary assistance.

- **1960s**: There is a noticeable and steady increase in the Fed's asset purchases after the US was removed from the gold standard.

- **2000 & 2001**: The response to two potentially destabilizing events, the Y2K scare and 9-11 tragedy, invoked unprecedented action from the Fed, although historic at that time, were miniscule when compared to 2008.

By now, it should be abundantly clear that today the Fed is exceedingly concerned about the health of our economy. Over seven years have passed since the turmoil of 2008, and yet the Fed fears raising rates above 0.0%, to even 0.25%, over concern of shocking a fragile economy. This should be quite disturbing. Anyone who gives the above charts even a cursory glance should recognize that something is out of whack. And that something is the health of our still-fragile economy, which each day is being artificially stimulated by a semi-private agency known as the Federal Reserve System.

"Over seven years have passed since the turmoil of 2008, and yet the Fed fears raising rates above 0.0%, to even 0.25%, over concern of shocking a fragile economy."

Fed Stimulus Also Came in the Form of Zero Interest Rates

Chart 2i reveals another form of historic Fed stimulus. It lowered the Fed Funds Rate in December 2008 to near zero, *and kept it at that level for seven years.* Never before had the Fed lowered this rate to zero. Never, in its 102 - year history. And it kept rates at zero for seven years. Combined with extreme money creation, I imagine it was very concerned about financial annihilation.

Chart 2i

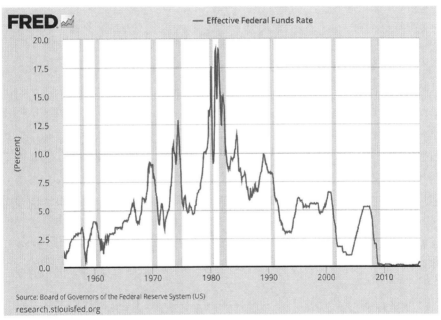

Source: Board of Governors of the Federal Reserve System (US)
research.stlouisfed.org

Board of Governors of the Federal Reserve System (US), Effective Federal Funds Rate [FED-FUNDS], retrieved from FRED, Federal Reserve Bank of St. Louis https://research.stlouisfed.org/fred2/series/FEDFUNDS, May 4, 2016.

"Never before had the Fed lowered this rate to zero. Never, in its 102 - year history."

Saving the US Economy from Another Great Depression

The Fed was prudent to respond to the crisis of 2008 in an historic manner. However, another seminal theory of this book contends it over did the money creation and hooked our economy on an addiction to Quantitative Easing that will be extremely hard to unwind.

In 2008, with the US economy in a panic, the US government and Federal Reserve were the only entities with a checkbook large enough to implement a massive financial stimulus to help compensate for a lack of consumer spending. Without their quick action and cash injection, the economy would have spiraled out of control.

Think what would have happened if Bear Sterns, AIG, Countrywide Financial, GM, Merrill Lynch, Washington Mutual, Citigroup, Fannie Mae & Freddie Mac, Wachovia and a host of other companies would have had to fend for themselves without the benefit of the Fed and its trillion dollar bailouts (remember TAF, TSLF, PDCF, AMLF, CPFF, TALF, Maiden Lane I, II, III?). They would likely have gone bankrupt or been sold to stronger firms at fire-sale prices, causing large layoffs and exacerbating the lack of consumer spending that led to the financial crisis. Chaos would have been the order of the day.

To underscore the panic, former US Treasury Secretary Timothy Geithner recalls:*

- "By September 18 (2008), panic was engulfing the system."
- "Even Goldman Sachs, the strongest of the investment banks, watched helplessly as half its $120 billion in

---

* *"Stress Test: Reflections on Financial Crises,"* Timothy Geithner liquidity evaporated in a week." (think about that for a moment ...)

- "I was scared, too. It looked like the system was going to collapse, taking down the strong firms along with the weak."
- "I thought we were looking at another global depression that would hurt billions of people."

One panic after another ensued. Writing about the events of November 23, 2008, Mr. Geithner continues:

- "The next domino in danger was Citigroup, a giant three times the size of Lehman Brothers and far more integral to the functioning of global markets."
- "Citi was still a mess, choking on mortgages on and off its balance sheet, with a highly vulnerable funding base."
- With Citi's stock price dropping below $4, down 93% from its 2006 peak, "Citi needed a solution that weekend."

Do you recall it being that bad? *"Another global depression"* kind of bad? A collapse that would *"take down the strong firms along with the weak"* sort of crisis, *"needing a solution that weekend?"*

I knew the financial system and stock markets were in a panic and prone to wild swings, but I did not realize they were this bad. Only those at the very top of the financial and political elite knew how dire the situation was at the time. They were correct to implement drastic measures, but perhaps they were influenced by the absence of stimulus from the 1930s Fed and kept the stimulus turned on far too long. Because of this, I believe we are now addicted to QE.

Chapter 2 Summary

Let's recap this chapter before we learn how the Federal Reserve System was born and how it became so powerful.

- The Fed enjoys the ability to create limitless money because the US is no longer tied to a gold standard. There is little hope of the US ever returning to a gold standard in our lifetime.

- Once our currency was no longer shackled to gold, Americans were able to live on credit and our Total Credit Market Debt grew at a record pace, from $1 trillion in the 1960s to over $65 trillion today.

- The US Current Account Balance, one of the most important economic developments of the 20th century, illustrates how US consumers were able to spend beyond their limits, recording an extraordinary trade deficit of $800 billion in 2006.

- Stagnant real incomes and a collapse of the housing market in 2007 led financially-extended consumers to significantly reduce their spending. This led to the first drop in Total Credit Market Debt since the 1960s and ushered in the Great Recession.

- The Fed rode to the rescue, injected historic amounts of cash into the financial system and bailed out many weak firms. The Fed's balance sheet alone ballooned from $900 billion to $4.5 trillion in just six years. The Fed Funds Rate was reduced to effectively zero for seven years.

- ~~We learned our lesson from an event described as "another global depression that would hurt billions of people", bringing politicians and Wall Street elite together to implement stringent measures to ensure this would never happen again.~~ *Never mind ... got carried away with this one.*

Throughout this book I refer to economic events occurring today that are so rare, they haven't occurred in decades. Even more frightening, we are witnessing many important events that have *never* been recorded in the history of our great country. The list is lengthy: historic Fed asset purchases, zero interest rates, our plunging US Current Account Balance and surging total credit market debt to name a few. We can now add the worst start to a year for the Dow and S&P500 indices *ever* in the history in our stock markets, with the downturn we witnessed in 2016.

If you are wondering "Why is this all happening now?" don't worry, I'm putting the puzzle together one piece at a time. We will also end with a discussion of investment strategies that may be prudent.

"... we are witnessing many important events that have never been recorded in the history of our great country."

But before we get there, it's important to learn how the Federal Reserve System was created and what led to it becoming the most powerful economic cartel in the world.

CHAPTER 3

How Did the Fed Get So Powerful?

The greatest discovery of my generation is that human beings can alter their lives by altering their attitudes.

William James

The US Central Bank, known as the Federal Reserve System, has grown to become the most powerful economic entity in the world. How was this quasi-private cartel formed?

Legendary financier J.P. Morgan was largely responsible for setting the wheels in motion to establish the Fed at the beginning of the 20th century. The Federal Reserve Act, which established the Federal Reserve, was passed into law on December 23, 1913. However, it was a banking crisis in 1907 that led Mr. Morgan to assemble the team who crafted and pushed this legislation through Congress. Let's begin with a summary of the events in 1907 which led to the creation of the Fed.

The Legendary Panic of 1907

In October 1907, long lines formed outside many New York banks as "a run on the banks" caused great concern and panic for financial institutions. In those days, there was no such thing as government protection of bank deposits, which today is known as FDIC insurance (Federal Deposit Insurance Corporation). When you deposited money in a bank, you essentially had its promise that it would return your money on demand. Banks accepted your deposit and lent the majority of this money to others at interest rates higher than what they paid on deposit accounts, earning a profit on the difference. Called *Fractional Reserve Banking*, only a small portion of these deposits were backed by cash in the vault and available for immediate withdrawal. The US no longer works under a fractional reserve banking system, as described in Appendix Two.

"When you deposited money in a bank, you essentially had its promise that it would return your money on demand."

When the solvency of a bank was called into question, nervous depositors lined up and demanded the return of their money. As lines formed at one bank, worried investors at other banks lined up at their bank, perpetuating a frenzy of uncertainty. Adding to this fear, payments on checks written from accounts at these banks were rejected when many banks and clearinghouses refused to clear checks drawn on "troubled" banks, a practice that led to failure of otherwise solvent banks.

These were precisely the events that unfolded in 1907. An attempt to control the stock price of the United Copper Company failed, resulting in its bankruptcy. This led to great instability on Wall Street, for both banking institutions and the New York Stock Exchange. In the end, numerous banks and trusts would fail, including the prestigious Knickerbocker Trust Company.*

---

* For more on this topic, read *The Panic of 1907* by Robert F. Bruner and Sean D. Carr. It is a concise and fascinating book on this important moment in our economic history.

As this crisis spiraled out of control, the entire stability of the stock exchange and New York financial firms were threatened. To re-live the sense of urgency and panic that permeated many banks at the time, allow Messrs. Bruner and Carr (authors of *The Panic of 1907*) to describe how one bank dealt with depositors demanding a return of their money:

The Trust Company of America was in imminent peril. Around the time that J. P. Morgan was hearing the report from Benjamin Strong, Oakleigh Thorne, president of the Trust Company, called the Corner and told J. Pierpont Morgan that his company's meager cash supply had dwindled to $1.2 million.

The run on the Trust Company had become formidable indeed, and Thorne was doubtful he could keep its doors open until the end of business at 3 pm. Nearly 1,200 depositors were assembled outside the Trust Company's main offices in lower Manhattan, grouped in a line snaking east to William Street and down to Exchange Place. In an attempt to stem the flow from his vaults, Thorne kept only two teller windows open all morning; he also arranged to have large piles of cash on view to reassure anxious depositors that the institution had ample reserves. But in a replay of the previous day's scenes at the Knickerbocker, worried customers, clerks, and office boys took up a desultory vigil to reclaim their (or their employer's) cash. Investors and depositors had lost faith in yet another prominent New York financial institution.

Twenty minutes later, Thorne called on Morgan again in a greater state of panic. His coffers were now down to

$800,000, and unless he could raise $3 million, he would have to close the Trust Company instantly. Morgan turned to the 10 trust company presidents in the room with him, whom he had called together earlier to address the widening panic. He suggested that each of them agree to loan $300,000 to the Trust Company of America. The president of the Farmers Loan & Trust Company took up the offer right away, but the meeting fell apart and devolved into a confused debate for another 20 minutes.

At about 1:45pm., Thorne again pleaded for aid. Now he had only $500,000 remaining. The trust officials continued to argue. In their view it was not their place to intervene, and they were prepared to abandon one of their own.

At 2:15pm., a committee from the Trust Company of America entered the room and reported they had only $180,000 left and they had decided to cease operations. "Well," Morgan exclaimed, "I don't see anything else to do." Exasperated by the temporizing of the trust companies, he abruptly dismissed the meeting. At the suggestion of his partner and close associate, George W. Perkins, Morgan summoned the presidents of the city's two largest banks: James Stillman of the National City Bank and George F. Baker of the First National Bank of New York. After opening a direct phone line to the offices of the Trust Company of America, Morgan told Oakleigh Thorne to come see him at once, bringing with him the most valuable securities held in his company's vaults.

Within minutes, the doors of Morgan's office were thrown open and in walked a long line of men with bags and boxes filled with securities owned by the Trust Company of

America. Stillman sat in an adjoining room where he maintained an open telephone line with the National City Bank. Morgan commanded a large table as Thorne and his clerks laid out the Trust Company's securities for the purpose of valuing them in exchange for a loan. Making notes on a pad as they went along, Morgan assessed the securities, and as he determined that enough collateral was available for an advance, he asked Stillman to have National City Bank send that amount in cash over to the Trust Company. Every few minutes, at Morgan's direction, money was carried in sacks and taken directly to the Trust Company's vaults. Morgan and his men proceeded in this way until $3 million had been delivered. The doors stayed open until 3 pm. and the Trust Company of America had been saved for a day.

J.P. Morgan

Legendary financier, savior of the US economy in 1907 and unofficial Father of the Federal Reserve System

This panic would be replayed 101 years later - on a much grander scale - as once venerable firms such as Bear Stearns, AIG, Lehman Brothers, Merrill Lynch and Wachovia desperately scrambled for their financial survival. While the numbers were larger, with information and assets delivered electronically in seconds, the fear and panic remained much the same. In both 1907 and 2008, survival of prestigious financial firms and our very economy was at stake.

After this last ditch effort temporarily saved the Trust Company of America, J. P. Morgan began to establish a much grander plan, as if to say, "We simply can't let this chaos happen again!" And he was right. Messrs. Bruner and Carr continue:

> As these emergency measures were undertaken on behalf of the Trust Company of America, there were signs that economic and financial conditions were deteriorating elsewhere. The Westinghouse Electric & Manufacturing Company had been placed in the hands of a receiver, the Pittsburgh Stock Exchange had suspended trading, and a run had begun at another leading New York trust institution, the Lincoln Trust Company. At the same time, the mayor of New York City, George B. McClellan (the son of the Civil War general), called for a conference with all his department heads when he learned that the city would be unable to pay its salaries and contractors.

And so the panic lurched from one institution to another, day after day, with the stakes ranging from small to intense. At one point, Mr. Morgan was told by the president of the New York Stock Exchange that they would have to close early unless a significant amount of money was offered on the stock exchange in a very short time. Fearing a larger catastrophe that even he would be unable to mend, Mr. Morgan promptly assembled the presidents of leading banks in his office and issued an ultimatum: Unless they raised $25 million within the next 12 minutes, at least 50 stock exchange houses would fail. Fourteen banks pledged $23.6 million within minutes and once again a debilitating crisis had been averted. For even a seasoned banker like Morgan, these events tested his financial and physical resolve. Something more permanent had to be done to shore up a shaky financial system.

"For even a seasoned banker like Morgan, these events tested his financial and physical resolve. Something more permanent had to be done to shore up a shaky financial system."

Naturally the stock market did not fare well with turmoil and uncertainty ruling the day. A chain reaction began as once strong companies, their stock pledged as collateral for loans, sank, causing loans to be called due to dwindling guarantees. J. P. Morgan was called upon once again to rescue a fragile financial environment, as the US Treasury held only $5 million in ready cash, effectively removing them as a financial resource. He drew upon his decades of considerable banking knowledge and developed a strategy that called for dramatic measures.

Mr. Morgan assembled New York's leading financial elite to his personal residence and literally locked the doors of his home until a solution was reached. Working virtually around the clock for the better part of two days, Mr. Morgan and his colleagues devised a plan to rescue companies deemed worthy of saving, while acknowledging others would have no choice but to fail. With formal agreements signed by supportive bank presidents to assist struggling financial institutions, the doors of Mr. Morgan's home were finally unlocked, allowing these weary financial luminaries to trudge home for a moment's rest.

This action finally brought lasting peace to financial markets, allowing time to heal the remaining minor wounds. Mr. Morgan, however, had one final task to orchestrate, forever elevating him to the pinnacle of America's financial elite. With his mind free to reflect on the harrowing months he just endured, he directed his efforts to sketching the rudimentary framework for today's Federal Reserve System.

"With his mind free to reflect on the harrowing months he just endured, he directed his efforts to sketching the rudimentary framework for today's Federal Reserve System."

What a monumental task this was. He outlined the structure for a cartel, imbued it with the illusion of being a government program, while granting private bankers direct access to the creation of US currency. How brilliant! Never again would a financial titan be called upon to coax financially strong firms to support their weakened brethren during times of duress. This agency would have the sole authority to control the creation of US currency, in any amount they deemed necessary, to support firms within their sphere of influence.

However, significant work remained, not only to craft the precise structure, but also to choreograph its formal acceptance in Washington.

Getting this structure officially recognized and legally adopted by Congress would require all the skills Mr. Morgan and his talented band of financiers could muster. It would also require the talents of seasoned politicians, pulling the necessary levers to allow this legislation to peak at just the right moment for passage into law.

"This agency would have the sole authority to control the creation of US currency, in any amount they deemed necessary, to support firms within their sphere of influence."

With the 1907 panic a distant memory in the public's eye, Mr. Morgan handed the outline for the Federal Reserve System to his trusted collaborators, sending them on a secret mission to his secluded retreat in Georgia to devise a strategy for its formal acceptance.

The Creature from Jekyll Island

Using the setting of a train station platform in New Jersey, Author G. Edward Griffin   began his extensive narrative about the creation of the Federal Reserve System in his Fed classic *The Creature from Jekyll Island.* Cloaked in secrecy on a cold and snowy night in 1910, the reader learns of a confidential journey aboard a luxurious rail car belonging to Rhode Island Senator Nelson Aldrich, one of the most powerful men in Washington.

While only six guests occupied this regal coach, few realized this historic 800 mile journey to a small island off the coast of Georgia would have far reaching financial implications for many decades to come. Jekyll Island, Georgia, had recently been purchased by J. P. Morgan and several business associates as a secluded retreat to hunt and escape the prying eyes of the media. Now the exclusive location would add a famous meeting to its resume, that of hosting the primary meeting that outlined the form and function of the Federal Reserve System, soon to be the most powerful central bank in the world.

The pedigree of these individuals was impeccable, and it was estimated they represented *one-fourth of the total wealth of the entire world.* Let that one sink in as we learn more about these travelers:

Nelson W. Aldrich, Republican "whip" in the Senate, chairman of the National Monetary Commission, business associate of J. P. Morgan, father-in-law to John D. Rockefeller, Jr.

Abraham Piatt Andrew, assistant secretary of the US Treasury and director of the US Mint.

Frank A. Vanderlip, president of National City Bank of New York, the most powerful bank at the time, representing William Rockefeller and the international investment banking house of Kuhn, Loeb & Company.

Henry P. Davison, senior partner of J. P. Morgan Company, president of Liberty National Bank and a founder of the Bankers Trust Company of New York.

Benjamin Strong, head of J. P. Morgan's Bankers Trust Company and first president of the Federal Reserve Bank of New York.

Paul M. Warburg, partner in Kuhn, Loeb & Company, representative of the Rothschild banking dynasty in England and France, and brother to Max Warburg who was head of the Warburg banking consortium in Germany and the Netherlands. Sworn in as a member of the first Federal Reserve Board on August 10, 1914.

This team combined politicians who helped grease the wheels of acceptance in Washington with bankers who ensured their interests were protected with ample government authority.

The name of this quasi-government agency had to be perfect as well. It had to invoke strength, appear to be part of the US government and infer deep financial reserves. How did they do? Consider this about the *Federal Reserve System*: It is not federal and there are no reserves. Although the structure includes twelve Federal Reserve Banks, they are not even banks, but corporations with stock held by the commercial banks which are members of the system. No wonder these early financial pioneers needed to muster such political talent! A heavy dose of obfuscation was the elixir necessary to carry out this important task.

"Consider this about the Federal Reserve System: It is not federal and there are no reserves."

Yet this distinguished alliance would find it difficult to ram this *System* through Congress. After spending nine days in Jekyll Island hammering out the details, it took over three years to get both sides of the political aisle, together with President Woodrow Wilson, to authorize the Federal Reserve Act. The political stunts and brinkmanship which led to the final passage could fill several pages, and remains a blight on shameful political posturing leading up to the vote (read below for an example).

The Gatekeeper: William Jennings Bryan

Several hurdles were shrewdly overcome on the journey toward political acceptance of the Fed, however a powerful gatekeeper stood firmly in the way of final passage. William Jennings Bryan, considered the most influential democrat in Congress, was vocal in his displeasure with the proposed act. But even he was no match for the skilled puppeteers orchestrating this denouement. A proverbial whisper in the ear of the president by one of our Jekyll Island travelers was all it took for the president to suggest Mr. Bryan reconsider his position. Observers were stunned by Mr. Bryan's complete change of heart as he enthusiastically threw his support behind this fine piece of legislation. In retrospect, perhaps it was the subsequent appointment of Mr. Bryan as President Wilson's next Secretary of State that had something to do with his new found enlightenment. Perhaps indeed.

It is often said that timing is everything, and our Fed architects had traveled too far to leave the timing of this historic vote to happenstance. The orchestrated moment they selected was brilliant ... just hours before the treasured Christmas recess for Congress! With Secretary of State Bryan wholeheartedly endorsing this profound piece of legislation, both houses of Congress quickly passed the Federal Reserve Act on December 22, 1913, and President Wilson signed it into law the very next day. Members of Congress could finally focus on the Christmas holiday, while the Jekyll Island lobbyists quietly rejoiced in their hard fought victory.

Interviewed a year later, Senator Aldrich could afford to be candid with his description of the real purpose behind his efforts. Quoted in a magazine called *The Independent*, the senator could finally speak his mind and revealed his true intentions, "Before the passage of this Act, New York bankers could only dominate the reserves of New York. Now, we are able to dominate the reserves of the entire country." The power of the Fed to create any amount of money and distribute it to third parties with little oversight or impunity was not lost on the senator. Unparalleled power was finally granted to a select group of private citizens to issue US currency for the primary benefit of Wall Street financial institutions. This would be clearly demonstrated by the actions of the Fed during and immediately after the Great Recession of 2008.

"Before the passage of this Act, New York bankers could only dominate the reserves of New York. Now, we are able to dominate the reserves of the entire country."

It's quite understandable why the approval process took so long. The structure of this new Federal Reserve System had to be explained to those voting it into law. The following is a synopsis of the form and function of the Fed. Can you imagine explaining this complex structure to a political colleague?

Simply Stated: The Operating Structure of the Federal Reserve System

The three main components of the Fed are:

- National Board of Governors
- 12 Regional Reserve Banks, and
- Federal Open Market Committee

The function of the **National Board of Governors** is to determine the system's monetary policy. The Board consists of seven members, who are appointed by the president and confirmed by the Senate.

One Board member, the chairman, controls the staff and is the single most powerful influence within the system.

The 12 **Regional Reserve Banks** hold cash reserves, supply currency to member banks, clear checks and act as a fiscal agent for the government. *They are corporations, not banks, with stock held by the commercial banks* that are members of the Fed. Member banks elect nine directors, including a Reserve Bank president; however, selection of the president and other officers is subject to veto by the National Board of Governors.

The **Federal Open Market Committee** implements the monetary policy established by the National Board. It manipulates interest rates and the money supply primarily by purchasing or selling US fixed-income securities, foreign securities or currencies. As previously referenced, it is believed the Committee extends this privilege to the purchase of US equities when necessary. Policy is formulated on a daily basis and monitored by the minute, with the Committee often intervening in the market to affect immediate changes.

The Open Market Committee consists of twelve members – seven members of the Board of Governors, president of the New York Regional Bank and four of the remaining eleven Reserve Bank presidents, who serve one-year terms on a rotating basis. Non-voting Reserve Bank presidents attend the meetings of the Committee, participate in discussions and contribute to the Committee's assessment of the economy and policy options.

Twenty-four bond dealers handle all sales of government securities. *Government agencies are forbidden from exchanging with each other without going through one of these twenty-four dealers, who earn commissions on each transaction.*

Interest rate and monetary policy decisions are made at secret meetings. Policy changes are released immediately after the meeting with minutes released three weeks later. Transcripts of the deliberations have been destroyed since 1970, when the Freedom of Information Act was passed.

The federal government does not own any stock in the Federal Reserve System. In that sense, the Fed is privately owned. However, this is misleading, as the stock owned by the commercial banks carries no proprietary interest, cannot be sold or pledged as collateral, and does not carry ordinary voting rights. Each bank is entitled to one vote, regardless of the amount of stock it holds. In reality, the stock is not evidence of "ownership," but simply certificates showing how much operating capital each bank has put into the System.

The Fed is not a government agency or a private corporation. It is subject to political control, yet it remains independent of political oversight. Perhaps the best way to describe the Federal Reserve System is to label it a cartel, as its organizational structure is uniquely designed to serve that end.

Acknowledgments to G. Edward Griffin author *The Creature from Jekyll Island.*

If you are fascinated by the creation and power of the Federal Reserve, I strongly suggest you read G. Edward Griffin's seminal account titled *The Creature from Jekyll Island.*

The US Treasury's Role in Alleviating Panics

As a reminder, the Fed uses *monetary* policy to strengthen and influence our economy, while the US Treasury uses *fiscal* policy to attempt the same. The Federal Reserve defines each as

> **Monetary policy** refers to actions taken by central banks to achieve macroeconomic policy objectives such as price stability, full employment and stable economic growth. In the United States, Congress established maximum employment and price stability as the macroeconomic objectives for the Federal Reserve; they are sometimes referred to as the Federal Reserve's dual mandate. Apart from these overarching objectives, Congress determined that operational conduct of monetary policy should be free from political influence. As a result, the Federal Reserve is an independent agency of the federal government.

> **Fiscal policy** is a broad term used to refer to the tax and spending policies of the federal government. Fiscal policy decisions are determined by the Congress and the Administration; the Federal Reserve plays no role in determining fiscal policy.

It is important to recognize the difference in authority between the Fed and the US Treasury when implementing monetary and fiscal policy. A poignant reminder occurred in the fall of 2008. Recall how the Fed was able to conjure QE1 and QE1+ in the secrecy of their financial lair to support financial markets. No government permission required, no hand wringing or political posturing. The result was over $1 trillion in financial fabrication decided during a closed-door meeting and distributed within a matter of months.

In contrast, the US Treasury doesn't have it so easy. To implement fiscal policy, politicians must provide approval to proceed. To illustrate this difference in authority, recall the events in the fall of 2008 amid significant financial turmoil.

For many, the desperate pleading on national TV by then Treasury Secretary Henry "Hank" Paulson underscored the severity of the situation. Several financial crises converged to plunge our economy into a recession. If help didn't arrive soon, a new depression was likely. AIG was one of several high profile companies on the brink of collapse. If allowed to fail, it would likely take others down with them, such as Goldman Sachs, a Wall Street darling with friends in high places.*

Over the years, AIG developed a steady stream of predictable cash flow by selling Credit Default Swaps on seemingly AAA-rated securities, only to discover during the financial crisis that a high percentage of these AAA securities were actually akin to junk bonds. Unable to find a buyer for some of its assets, AIG was on the verge of bankruptcy and turned to the only lenders of last resort, the US government and Federal Reserve, for help.

This is where a significant difference between the Fed and US Treasury is revealed. Even though the Fed possessed no regulatory authority over AIG, it nonetheless provided $85 billion in financial assistance with a sweep of its invisible hand. No government approval required, no contentious discussion in Congress nor approval by the president. As if to say, "AIG, you need some money? Will $85 billion help? Well, here it is!"

---

* It was not unusual for former Goldman executives to take high-profile government jobs. In fact, the sitting Treasury Secretary during the crisis, Hank Paulson, was a former Goldman chairman and CEO.

It was not so easy for Hank Paulson and the Treasury. Recognizing that AIG, Goldman Sachs and several venerable firms (Citigroup, Bank of America, JP Morgan and Wells Fargo to name a few) were in need of government assistance, the Troubled Asset Relief Program (TARP) was conceived. $700 billion was needed to stabilize these firms, however Mr. Paulson was required to ask permission before funds could be released. Even as Treasury secretary, he could not just wield his electronic checkbook and create $700 billion with a stroke of his pen. Time was of the essence, and Congress did not have the luxury to dither. Days, not weeks, were all politicians had to grant the Treasury secretary permission to fabricate and disperse the $700 billion.

Yet dither they did. The first bill authorizing the treasury to spend $700 billion was defeated in the House on Monday, September 29th. The Dow promptly fell 778 points or 7%. It took the entire week and a falling stock market for the House to vote again and finally pass the bill on Friday, October 3rd. Initially, an uncertain market sent the Dow lower by 800 points, only to recover most of these losses once passage was announced.

Notice the difference? The US Treasury had to ask for *permission* to spend $700 billion on a bailout. Congress had to *approve* the spending and the president had to *sign* the bill into law.

The Fed, on the other hand, a private entity, is free from such trivial procedures. If it wants to conjure $85 billion to help AIG, a closed-door session, or perhaps a phone call to members of the Fed is all that's necessary. Poof! $85 billion magically appears for the benefit of AIG. As noted in Chapter One, the Fed increased its balance sheet by $3.6 trillion during the crisis without approval from Congress or the White House. Thank you J. P. Morgan, for designing such a unique institution with an unlimited checkbook to spring into action during times of crisis. While this power is

vital and **wise** during times of panic, it's easy to see how this can also be detrimental to our economy. Some believe the QE injections were continued far beyond the logical point required to stabilize our economy. Perhaps the return of volatility to the financial markets substantiates this theory and suggests global economies are indeed addicted to QE.

Gazing into my opaque crystal ball, it appears unlikely the Treasury will seek approval for additional fiscal policy before the 2016 presidential election, unless the economy really takes a turn for the worse. The Fed will also be reluctant to implement QE4, or adjust the Fed Funds Rate in 2016, because of the election. However, if a stock market sell-off is significant, or financial institutions are threatened, then the Fed will likely be forced to act. For the good of the country, naturally, and not to bail out troubled financial institutions and support rising stock prices once again (sarcasm intended).

Chapter 3 Summary

- J. P. Morgan, the legendary financier, orchestrated the rescue of the stock market and financial institutions in 1907. Using his influence and expertise, he directed cash infusions from strong, private, institutions to the weakened brethren of his choosing. Without this aid, many financial institutions would have failed. The US Treasury was financially inept due to modest financial reserves. Read *The Panic of 1907* by Robert F. Bruner and Sean D. Carr for an exceptional accounting of this event.

- Author G. Edward Griffin's Fed classic *The Creature from Jekyll Island* describes how the Fed was created and reveals its form and function. A better understanding of this institution, defined as an economic cartel, is vital to comprehending how this key player coordinates economic activity on the world's financial stage. Add this book to your reading list as well.

- By creating the Federal Reserve System, Congress intended to eliminate severe financial crises that had periodically swept the nation, especially the type of financial panic that occurred in 1907.

- The Fed uses monetary policy to affect change, while the US Treasury utilizes fiscal policy. The Fed can act unilaterally, while the Treasury must ask Congress for approval.

- Granting authority to an agency like the Federal Reserve System to act decisively during times of panic is wise and prudent. However, the excessive use and extent of its intervention is troubling, especially if our global economy is now addicted to QE.

The money printing game is not unique to the US and has gone global. China, Japan and the European Union didn't want to be left behind, especially if a little money creation can boost economies. Chapter Four will take a peek at their balance sheets and see how resourceful they have been since the Great Recession shook the world's economy.

CHAPTER **4**

It's a Global Addiction

Things may come to those who wait ... but only the things left behind by those who hustle.

Abraham Lincoln

Global Central Bankers Must Do Their Part

Ever wonder why geese heading south for the winter fly in a "V" pattern? (Better yet, wonder why I'm talking about geese in a chapter about global QE? Stick with me!)

There are several reasons why geese fly in a V pattern and it has to do with saving energy and working together. During long flights, geese fly on both sides of the leader in order to benefit from

an uplift created by the flapping of the wings directly in front of them. By doing so, it is estimated the entire flock can add as much as 71% more distance to their travels. When the lead goose tires, it moves to the back and the next in line takes its place. Flying in formation also assists with the flock's communication and coordination. Fighter pilots often use this same technique when flying in formation for many of the same reasons.

Now back to global QE ...

Recovering from the depths of the Great Recession required the US Federal Reserve System to coordinate a global response. Like our flock of geese, asset prices can rise higher for a prolonged period of time when all major central banks work together. Their collective "lift" can take the form of lower interest rates, hints of easy monetary policies or ultimately the direct intervention of additional QE. After the Great Recession, the Fed called upon China, Japan and Eurozone central bankers to play a major role in the global recovery. Whenever a sustained rally in stocks appeared overseas, it was likely supported by the action of a central bank. When one banker grew tired of taking the lead on QE, another stepped in with its version to "goose" the markets higher (I just couldn't resist that one!).

"After the Great Recession, the Fed called upon China, Japan and Eurozone central bankers to play a major role in the global recovery."

When central bankers get desperate, they even resort to buying stocks to achieve desired results. China's central bank reportedly buys stocks with their bank assets, while Japanese central bankers are clearly not bashful as they routinely publicize the amount of stocks they buy with QE assets. Unfortunately, the economic situation in Japan is so dire that buying Japanese bonds will not move the economic needle anymore, forcing the Bank of Japan (BOJ, Japan's central bank) to add the purchase of stocks to its QE quiver. Buying Japanese stock ETFs grew so prolific, according to Bloomberg news, that the BOJ now owns more than half of the nation's market for exchange-traded stock funds. Will this strategy be exported to the US? Perhaps. Some even believe it is underway in the US already, but few know for sure as our Fed isn't as forthcoming as Japan.

"When central bankers get desperate, they even resort to buying stocks to achieve desired results."

The following chart is a great way to continue our discussion on international QE as it illustrates global asset creation since the Great Recession (ROW refers to the Rest of the World and FX, short for Forex, refers to the global foreign exchange market). Notice the extensive and pronounced use of QE, especially since 2008.

Chart 4a

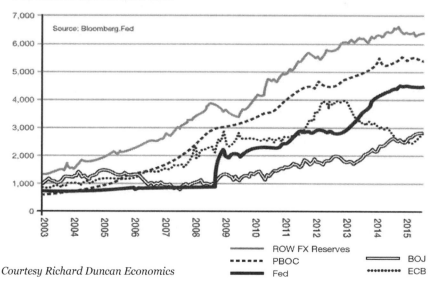

The Total Assets of the Four Largest Central Banks plus the FX Reserves of the Rest of the World
US$ billions, 2003 to June 2015

Courtesy Richard Duncan Economics

The shape of the Fed's QE efforts should be familiar to readers by now. The upward trajectory is quite pronounced as QE1 was initiated in 2008. The steady and deliberate advance in 2013 echoes the stock market response to the Fed's aggressive QE3+ monetary policy.

What many readers may find interesting is these herculean efforts by the Fed only garnered them second place in the global QE race as China led all participants with its unwavering dedication to propping up its slowing economy. A closer look into China's response to the Great Recession reveals a fascinating story of its determination to keep its population happy, at literally any cost.

"China led all participants with its unwavering dedication to propping up its slowing economy."

How China Fooled the World

Robert Peston is no stranger to China and has been intrigued with its economy for many years. As a seasoned journalist reporting for BBC, he produced exceptional documentaries on this subject.*

Mr. Peston recalled when the US created the Great Recession with our banking crisis, sending shock waves around the world. The abrupt halt in world trade had a significant

---

* Watch Robert Peston's 3-minute documentary on this subject at: http://www.bbc.com/news/business-26225205 or indulge yourself with the 46-minute version at: http://www.bbc.com/news/world-asia-34261550

impact on China, our largest trading partner, as reported in his documentary:

> Well in the autumn of 2008, after the collapse of Lehman, there was a sudden and dramatic shrinkage of world trade. And that was catastrophic for China, whose growth was largely generated by exporting to the rich West all that stuff we craved. When our economies went bust, we stopped buying - and almost overnight, factories turned off the power, all over China.
>
> I visited China at the time and witnessed mobs of poor migrant workers packing all their possessions, including infants, on their backs and heading back to their villages. It was alarming for the government, and threatened to smash the implicit contract between the ruling Communist Party and Chinese people - namely, that they give up their democratic rights in order to become richer.
>
> So with encouragement from the US government (we interviewed the then US Treasury Secretary, Hank Paulson), the Chinese government unleashed a stimulus programme of mammoth scale: £400bn of direct government spending, and an instruction to the state-owned banks to "open their wallets" and lend as if there were no tomorrow.

How big was this massive spending program? According to Mr. Peston, it was an ambitious building program "on the scale we haven't seen since Egypt's Pharaohs," funded by trillions of dollars of debt. China began building a new skyscraper every five days, adding 30 new airports, constructing new metro systems in 25 cities, including 6,000 miles of high-speed railway. Roadways were not neglected, as 26,000 miles of highway and three of the longest bridges in the world were built. All in just the last six years. To put this in perspective, the total length of interstate highways in the US stands near 48,000 miles, second to China, with our system dating back to 1956 under President Eisenhower. China effectively built more than half the US highway capacity in the past six years alone.

It is customary for Chinese construction crews to literally work around the clock. To complete a train station in the city of Wuhan, 500 workers were divided in four teams laboring over three shifts, as one of just 10,000 ongoing construction projects in this city. Elsewhere, a 30-story hotel was completed in just *two weeks* (watch this amazing documentary at https://www.youtube.com/watch?v=F1ZsVUB_-qg).

China's infrastructure is just as impressive. The Wuhan Iron and Steel plant, located along the banks of the Yangtze River, produces over 40 million tons of product each year. How much is that? At this rate, they fabricate enough steel to build an Eiffel Tower ... *every two hours.*

Who pays for this massive spending program? Borrowing a page from our Fed's playbook when it infused a weak economy with fabricated currency, China quickly became a seasoned pro at the game. Charlene Chu, of Fitch Ratings, an international rating agency, commented on China's incredible increase in deficit spending, "Most people are aware we've had a credit boom in China but they don't know the scale. At the beginning of all of this in 2008, the Chinese banking sector was roughly $10 trillion in size. Right now it's in the order of $24 to $25 trillion."

She continued, "That incremental increase of $14 to $15 trillion is the equivalent of the entire size of the US commercial banking sector, which took more than a century to build. So that means China will have replicated the entire US system in the span of half a decade. Mathematically, there is no way to grow out of this problem when credit is twice the size of the economy and growing twice as fast."

> **"Mathematically, there is no way to grow out of this problem when credit is twice the size of the economy and growing twice as fast."**

Quite a sobering statement, given China is the world's second largest economy. If you are curious about China's rapid building boom, search the Internet or YouTube for numerous stories and videos on China's fabled "ghost cities" and "The Great Mall of China." It may give you a better appreciation of why nearly ten million Chinese homes are built each year with estimates suggesting 15% remain vacant.

When Mr. Peston asked a local musician about the explosive growth he witnessed in China, the citizen commented, "It is good for government officials and some rich men, but it is not good for normal Chinese. The poor stay poor, the rich get more rich." Sound familiar?

Tracking China's QE Program

One frustrating issue regarding China is the lack of government transparency regarding its economic efforts. While the Federal Reserve freely shares numerous charts on a variety of financial topics at their FRED website (Federal Reserve Bank of St. Louis https://research.stlouisfed.org), it's difficult to gather similar data on China's economic development. However, with the assistance of a very insightful economist, Richard Duncan, and his *Macro Watch* economic blog and video program, we get a glimpse into this economy with valuable commentary. The following chart depicts how China is funding the growth we just described:

Chart 4b

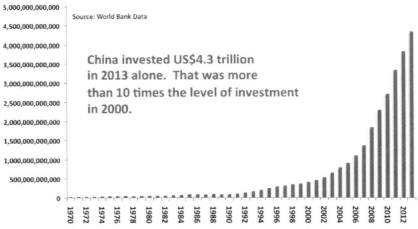

China: Investment
Gross Fixed Capital Formation (current US$), 1970 to 2013

China invested US$4.3 trillion in 2013 alone. That was more than 10 times the level of investment in 2000.

Source: World Bank Data

Courtesy Richard Duncan Economics

What accounts for this explosive growth in capital formation, defined as the purchase of buildings and equipment to increase production capacity? Perhaps the answer is a proud Chinese communist government concerned for the people's welfare. For years, a communist government encouraged workers to migrate from their farms to cities where jobs and opportunity were plentiful.

During the good times, workers were busy producing goods for sale around the world. Their legendary work ethic and low personal demands made for an ideal pool of skilled manual labor. When factories fell silent in 2008, these same workers were unable to survive in the city without gainful employment. Returning to their farms was a viable option as many packed their belongings and prepared to leave the city. Viewing this as a failure of government policies, the communists created an amazing building boom to keep these workers busy (hence the dramatic growth in capital formation). Even if it meant building bridges to nowhere and ghost cities the size of Philadelphia.

Funding this amazing building boom was an easy task for China's central bank (People's Bank of China's, PBOC) given its ability to create trillions in currency through bank lending programs.

We see this money creation reflected in the growth of bank loans in China, Chart 4c. While China's government stimulated its economy with $590 billion in spending, China's state-owned banks were directed to lend trillions more to fuel the rampant growth previously described.

Chart 4c

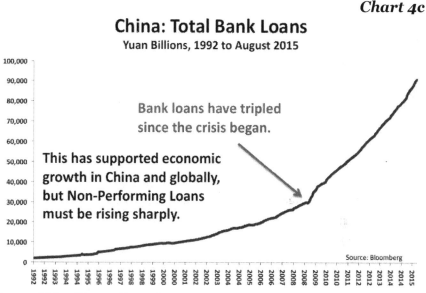

China: Total Bank Loans
Yuan Billions, 1992 to August 2015

Courtesy Richard Duncan Economics

The economic paradigm shift that created this incredible building boom remains a global phenomenon, with charts like the growth of Total Foreign Exchange Reserves (Chart 4d) reminding us of the exceptional growth of economic capital (represented by foreign exchange reserves, bank loans, fiat money creation, etc.). This is fiat money creation on a scale the world has never seen before, and at least seventy-percent of these reserves are held in US dollars.

"This is fiat money creation on a scale the world has never seen before"

Chart 4d

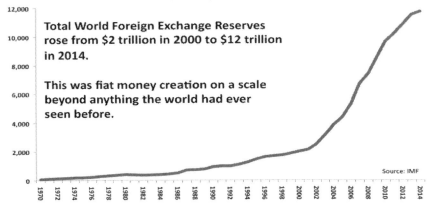

Total Foreign Exchange Reserves
US$ billions, 1970 to 2014

Total World Foreign Exchange Reserves rose from $2 trillion in 2000 to $12 trillion in 2014.

This was fiat money creation on a scale beyond anything the world had ever seen before.

Source: IMF

Courtesy Richard Duncan Economics

As we have come to expect, the Chinese political elite are quick to react when troubles surface in China, while keeping a modicum of secrecy. The Chinese have demonstrated an ability to stimulate its economy in a variety of traditional ways - whether it's spending $590 billion, creating money or directing state-owned banks to lend trillions to jump-start a flagging economy. Now, they are learning another way to implement QE from the Japanese (and perhaps our Fed) by purchasing stocks in the Chinese stock market.

Early reports in 2016 from Bloomberg suggest Chinese - controlled funds bought stocks in its stock market in response to a horrific start to the year for investment markets. This is yet another reason I believe most global central banks will resort to buying stocks and implementing other extreme QE measures when an economy suffers severe turbulence.

To see where this exceptional amount of credit spending by China and the US may lead, Japan's economy may provide a glimpse into our economic future.

Beyond the Point of No Return

Fans of the *Phantom of the Opera* recognize this title, and it serves as an ominous reference to Japan and their numerous attempts to kick-start a struggling economy dating back to the 1990s. Japan's central bank is known for its aggressive implementation of a variety of QE initiatives, with some programs reaching a point of saturation. Are they reaching a point of no return, where each successive QE scheme comes with a diminishing effect? Like the Phantom as he pilots his craft beneath the opera house, perhaps Japan is being seduced by a siren's song of easy money as it drifts down a dark and misty byway beyond its own point of no return.

Do you remember the glorious days of Japan in the 1980s? They went on quite the spending spree, buying iconic US treasures such as Rockefeller Center and the Pebble Beach Golf Course, while gobbling up pricy Hawaiian real estate in 1987 with their frenzied buying. The Nikkei stock market was also on a tear, rising four-fold in just five years (from 10,000 in 1984 to as high as 39,000 in 1989). At that time, a survey of institutional investors showed the majority of them did not believe the Nikkei was overvalued. What could possibly go wrong?

Well, for starters ... everything. Japanese official decided to tighten monetary policy as they grew concerned about the possibility of asset bubbles. Ya think? The Nikkei stock market was an early casualty, plunging nearly fifty-percent in 1990 from 39,000 to 20,000. From there, it trickled lower, falling an additional twenty-five percent toward 15,000 by 1992 and below 10,000 numerous times in the new century. This, from a country once the second largest GDP center in the world, and still ranked number three today.

Chart 4e

JAPAN NIKKEI 225 STOCK MARKET INDEX

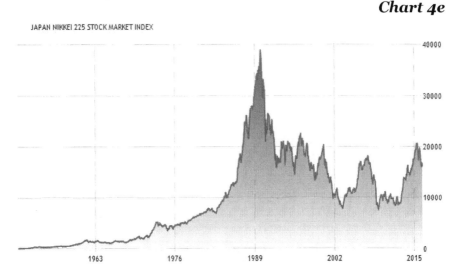

Courtesy Tradingeconomics.com

What have its officials done since 1990 to stimulate a sluggish economy? Plenty. To be fair, Japan has significant demographic headwinds to contend with, most notably an aging population.* Excellent books have been written on Japan's lost decade, therefore I will limit my observation to a few key economic observations.

Japan's Anemic GDP Growth

As a reminder, Gross Domestic Product (GDP) is the monetary value of all finished goods and services produced by a country. It is a popular method of gauging the economic health of a country,

---

* According to *Euromonitor International*, Japan has the highest percentage of citizens over 65 in the world, making up more than 20 percent of its population.

especially if a prolonged increase or decrease is detected. In the US, according to *Trading Economics*, GDP has averaged 3.25% from 1947 to 2015, a testament to our number-one standing as the most robust economy in the world.

As Chart 4f shows, Japan's annual growth rate has stagnated since the late 1980s, averaging just 0.49% from 1980 to 2015. For comparison, the world's number four GDP country, Germany, averaged 1.32% from 1992 to 2015. Number two China's GDP figures are not provided, as I believe they are unreliable due to the perception of questionable figures released over the years from an enthusiastic government.

Chart 4f

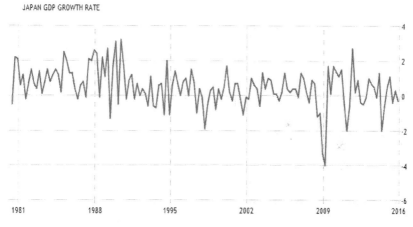

JAPAN GDP GROWTH RATE

SOURCE- WWW.TRADINGECONOMICS.COM | CABINET OFFICE, JAPAN

Courtesy Tradingeconomics.com

Japan's central bank, the Bank of Japan (BOJ), continues to feed its economy with extreme levels of financial stimulus. The results, however, may be waning as Japan has already experienced two recessions since 2012; this, from the world's third largest GDP and an innovator in QE financing. Is its economy finally immune to the effects of QE? Hopefully not, for its sake.

The Japanese Bond Market, or Lack Thereof

With the BOJ plucking $80 trillion yen a year from thin air to purchase Japanese government bonds, concerned economists predict the demise of the Japanese bond market by 2027. While it is unlikely the BOJ will continue this extreme rate of bond purchases, it is nevertheless striking that the bond market in the third most prosperous country in the world is on a path toward extinction, according to Ryutaro Kono, chief Japan economist in Tokyo at BNP Paribas. With the BOJ owning over thirty-percent of all Japanese government bonds, Mr. Kono stated "The JGB (Japan Government Bond) market is nearly extinct thanks to the BOJ's aggressive stimulus."

"The JGB market is nearly extinct thanks to the BOJ's aggressive stimulus."

Mr. Kono, voted the number-one economist by *Nikkei Veritas* magazine in six of the past seven years, continued, "There will no longer be a market when a single player holds a forty-percent share. The BOJ will not be able to sustain the pace of expansion in the monetary base by around the middle of 2016." When demand for a bond is high, the yield on that bond typically falls, as reflected in the historically low yield on the Japanese 10-year government bond chart below.*

As if to exacerbate a low-yield environment, the BOJ announced a first-ever negative interest rate policy in January 2016, ultimately driving down JGB yields to below zero percent. That means bond

---

* To learn more about the effect of interest rates on bond prices, read *Bond Basics 101* on page 122.

Chart 4g

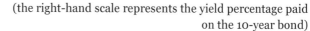

(the right-hand scale represents the yield percentage paid
on the 10-year bond)

JAPAN GOVERNMENT BOND 10Y

Courtesy Tradingeconomics.com

holders earn no interest for ten years and receive less of their capital when the bond matures. Amazing. This prompted another first - the subsequent cancellation of the March 2016 sale of 10-year JGBs amid expectations of below-zero yields. The negative yield announcement quickly took its toll on existing bonds, as nearly 70% of the JGBs in the market reported negative yields, according to the Japan Securities Dealers Association.

If you are concerned the BOJ will run out of options once it stops buying government bonds or driving down yields, don't worry! The BOJ has already aggressively deployed another weapon in its QE arsenal: buying Japanese stocks with fabricated money.

Japan's central bank is candid about its purchase of Japanese stocks and already owns more than *half of the nation's market for exchange-traded stock funds* in the world's third largest stock market, according to Bloomberg Business. Moreover, they plan to buy plenty more. With so much buying by a central bank, no wonder Japan's stock market surged in recent years, rising over 130% from 2012 to 2015.

"The BOJ already owns more than half of the nation's market for exchange-traded stock funds*"*

Chart 4h

Japan's ETF Whale

■ Bank of Japan ETF Holdings   ■ Entire ETF Market Assets

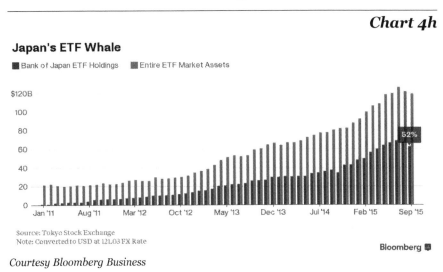

Source: Tokyo Stock Exchange
Note: Converted to USD at 121.03 FX Rate

Bloomberg

Courtesy Bloomberg Business

What could go wrong with a central bank buying stocks to prop up its economy? Here's what Masaru Hamasaki, head of the investment information department at Amundi Japan said, "At a fundamental level, I don't support the idea of central banks buying ETFs or equities. Unlike bonds, equities never redeem. That means they will have to be sold at some point, which creates market risk."

When your back is against the wall and you want to keep the economy and politicians happy, you turn to these extreme measures in order to keep your job. And keeping one's job as a policymaker in Japan is not an easy task. To underscore the legislative turmoil this industrious country has endured over the past 40 years, the current political leader, Shinzo Abe is now Japan's longest serving prime minister since the 1970s, with three years of continuous service to his credit. Wow, a 40-year record is broken when the prime minister of the world's third largest economy keeps his job for three straight years. For some reason, I don't find this comforting.

So, with China borrowing and building like there's no tomorrow and Japan on a mission to own all of the country's stocks and bonds, with a turnstile in the office of prime minister, can we find sanity in Europe?

A Dysfunctional Eurozone Central Bank

Ahhh ... isn't it nice to have a central bank with complete control over a nation's currency? With the ability to create money without a stringent approval process or someone looking over your shoulder? The US and China enjoy this luxury and Japan has a seasoned political veteran employing "Abe-nomics" to keep its economy off life support. So, what about the Eurozone? It has Germany, the world's fourth largest GDP engine firing on all cylinders to keep its economy humming. How is the Eurozone economy performing and how much stimulus does it inject into its collective of 19 member nations?

The answer requires us to delve deeper into the structure of this unique alliance of coalition governments. First, let's take another look at Chart 4a, the Total Assets of The Four Largest Central Banks. Do you notice how relatively smooth the trajectory is for all but one of the lines? What's up with the ECB line? Why does it look so haphazard compared to the Rest of the World (ROW), China, US and Japan?

Chart 4a *(repeat)*

**The Total Assets of the Four Largest Central Banks
plus the FX Reserves of the Rest of the World**
US$ billions, 2003 to June 2015

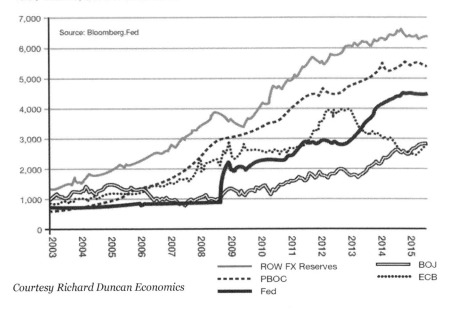

Courtesy Richard Duncan Economics

The answer lies in the fundamental makeup of Europe's "super" central bank and its unwieldy structure. The Eurozone is a monetary union consisting of 19 of 28 European Union member states. These 19 countries adopted the Euro as their common currency, while the remaining nine countries use their own national currencies. The Euro was born in 1992 when the Maastricht Treaty was adopted and introduced into circulation between 1999 and 2002 as the official Eurozone currency. It quickly grew to be the second largest reserve currency as well as the second most traded currency in the world, after the US dollar. Not bad for a fledgling currency.

---

*"The Eurozone is a monetary union consisting
of 19 of 28 European Union member states."*

The European Central Bank (ECB) administers the monetary policy for these 19 countries using the Euro, which is where the challenge of a cohesive strategy begins.

Think of the ECB as a "super" central bank presiding over 19 autonomous member countries, each with its own mini central bank. As can be expected, these member states have their own strengths and weaknesses that ebb and flow over time. Sometimes problems occur due to the absence of a forgiving attitude of camaraderie among these Eurozone nations, unlike the cohesion enjoyed within the United States. This important difference results in a haphazard and sometimes dysfunctional unified monetary policy in Europe.

Take the US as an example of a unified monetary policy for 50 member states. Some states may experience economic stress from time to time, while others enjoy periods of economic prosperity (think of a strong Alaska, Texas and North Dakota when oil revenues are high, and a weak California when a debilitating drought wreaks havoc on the world's most productive agricultural valley). Despite these temporary economic contrasts between states, the US gladly adheres to a unified monetary policy guided by the Fed, banks and US Treasury. Each state does not have its own mini central bank and gladly yields this power to the Fed.

Europe's super central bank (the ECB) does not enjoy this luxury. It must shepherd the 19 individual mini central banks, each with its own unique personality and priorities, to arrive at a unified decision on a macro monetary policy. Months of politicking, gentle persuasion and compromise are reflected in the jagged and haphazard ECB FX line in Chart 4a. To illustrate this tumultuous process, let's explore how long it took the ECB president to announce and initiate his first version of QE.

A Battle between the North and South

You may be thinking of the 1860s war in the US for the survival of a young and fragile collection of states with differing ideas of how to run a unified country. Strong differences of opinion resulted in significant bloodshed before a lasting compromise was reached. Europe had its own battle between the north and south, thankfully without bloodshed, exemplified by a 2015 showdown between Germany (a strong northern country) and Greece (a weakened southern country). This feud threatened the very stability of the Euro member states as Greece considered its own succession with a return to its former currency, the Drachma.

Recalling Chart 1a, it was September 2012 when Mario Draghi, president of the ECB, famously announced he would "do whatever it takes" to protect the Eurozone from collapse. Specifically, he stated "Within our mandate, the ECB is ready to do whatever it takes to preserve the euro. And believe me, it will be enough." On the day of the news, markets in the US and across Europe cheered, sending the S&P500 index higher, the London FTSE 100 up 1.4%, the IBEX in Spain up 6.0%, the Italy FTSE MIB up 5.6% and the Paris CAC 40 up 4.0%. "Super Mario" was acclaimed throughout the land!

But this was merely a *promise* of future support. At that time, the ECB had just completed its $1+ trillion of low interest loans to Eurozone banks (the LTRO program) and this announcement was its promise to continue feeding the addiction of cheap money to banks across Europe ... at some later date.

However, it would be a long time before Europe's QE was actually implemented.

On December 4, 2014, over two years after the memorable "whatever it takes" comment, the ECB was *still debating details* regarding implementation of its first government bond-buying program. The markets were decidedly disappointed when the late-afternoon announcement revealed that QE1 would be delayed once again, until early 2015. Who says QE doesn't have a direct effect on the markets? Notice the sharp downturn in the chart lines below and the corresponding lower stock indices on the afternoon of the announcement:

Chart 4i

NEXT 150 IDX	2,056.14	-0.270 %	-5.650
FTSE 100	6,679.37	-0.550 %	-37.260
XETRA DAX	9,851.35	-1.210 %	-120.440
CAC 40	4,323.89	-1.550 %	-67.970
FTMIB	19,424.38	-2.770 %	-553.940
IBEX 35	10,619.90	-2.350 %	-256.000

Photograph: Thompson Reuters, Courtesy Guardian News and Media Limited

To underscore the hand-wringing the ECB president endured during months of negotiations, the *Guardian News and Media* recounted the difficulties in gaining a consensus on that frustrating day:

Cracks are appearing in the governing council

The European Central Bank has resisted launching a quantitative easing programme today, despite the weak eurozone economy.

The ECB has hardened up its desire to expand its balance sheet back to 2012 levels - taking it from €2 trillion today back to €3 trillion. But that decision was not unanimous; even some members of the executive council refused to back Draghi, he revealed.

"Yes indeed, 'intended' is different from 'expected'. It's not simply an expectation, it's an intention, it's not yet a target, it's something in between. It was the vast majority of the members of the Governing Council, but obviously it was not unanimous."

But that might not stop QE. Draghi insisted that the ECB could launch a new stimulus package without unanimity:

"It's an important monetary policy measure, it can be designed, I believe, to have consensus. But we have to remember that we have a mandate, and as I said before, we don't tolerate prolonged deviations from our mandate."

Draghi also rejected the notion that European treaties barred the ECB from buying government debt.

Poor Super Mario. Oh, how he must long for the real super-powers of our Fed! Just imagine the ease of closing the doors, huddling with twelve trusted friends, then announcing the next day you decided to spend $1 trillion to push asset prices higher? How wonderful it must be to wield such power! No back-door deals, no gentle persuasion, no thoughts of "was I out of my mind to accept this job?" Just close the door and decide in two days … not two years.

There you have it. A synopsis of global central banks, each with its unique challenges, but a common goal: Do whatever it takes to stimulate their respective economies, even if it means employing unconventional methods with the potential of disastrous and debilitating longer-term results.

Chapter 4 Summary

- To recover from the Great Recession, the Federal Reserve worked in concert with global central bankers (China, Japan and the Eurozone) to inflate asset prices.

- Chart 4a, *Total Assets of the Four Largest Central Banks*, reveals pronounced and dramatic asset growth from 2007. The Eurozone is the only central bank with a haphazard and erratic history of asset growth.

- China felt the pain of the Great Recession and implemented an astonishing spending program financed by over $14 trillion of deficit spending. An analyst warned, "Mathematically, there is no way to grow out of this problem when credit is twice the size of the economy and growing twice as fast."

- Bank loans in China have tripled since 2008, representing fiat money creation on a scale the world has never seen before, according to economist Richard Duncan.

- Japan is fighting many economic battles, such as anemic GDP growth and an aging population. Its solution is to gobble up the majority of outstanding Japanese government bonds and stock ETFs on the Japanese stock exchange, while sending government bond yields below zero.

- The Eurozone is challenged by its design - 19 of 28 European Union member states use the euro currency under the leadership of Mario Draghi, the central bank president. He oversees a super-central bank composed of 19 individual central banks and finds it far more difficult than his US, Chinese and Japanese counterparts to implement a cohesive economic strategy.

The most influential central bank on the planet, the Federal Reserve System, combines the ability to create Federal Reserve Notes with the prestige of the US dollar as the world's premium reserve currency. Some economists and financial experts believe the days of the US dollar's world dominance are numbered, forecasting a slow and eventually painful death. Chapter Five believes this may be a bit premature, as King Dollar is here it stay. Let's find out why.

CHAPTER 5

King Dollar, for the Foreseeable Future

*Whether you believe you can or can't
do something, you're right!*

Henry Ford

In 2015, the 16-cylinder, 1,500 horsepower Bugatti Chiron was unveiled as the world's fastest production car with a top speed estimated at 288mph. Retail buyers of the Chiron, however, were likely disappointed to learn their cars were limited to a lower top speed, thanks to a device called a speed limiter or "governor." The vehicle you drive is probably prevented from traveling at its top speed as well, due to the use of a governor to prevent the car from accelerating beyond safety limits.

Photo courtesy of Bugatti Automobiles

Besides an awesome picture of the Bugatti and interesting fact about your car, what does this have to do with a book on QE?

Everything. When the US dollar was decoupled from gold in 1971, a governor that prevented excessive money printing was essentially removed.

Chapter Two reminds us that the 1944 Bretton Woods Agreement formally acknowledged the US dollar as the world's reserve currency. As such, the dollar was the standard to which every other currency was pegged. Most international transactions were denominated in US dollars, even when the US was not part of the deal. It also established a fixed exchange rate for the dollar and gold at $35 per ounce, essentially installing a "governor" on the government's ability to issue excessive amounts of currency. When our government found this restraint cumbersome, the US decoupled the dollar from gold in 1971, allowing the unlimited creation of currency. Since then, the intrinsic value of the dollar has weakened appreciatively due to inflation.

By how much?

Since 1971, the dollar has lost over 80% of its purchasing power. For a perspective, it is estimated that $16.63 of 1971 dollars would buy $100 in items today. To combat this erosion and preserve purchasing power, the Fed targets a modest two percent inflation each year, which is generally okay as long as wages and income rise at the same or higher rate.

However, purchasing power has eroded since 1913, while inflation-adjusted wages for the middle class has stagnated for twenty-five years (remember Chart 2e?). This is a problem some experts fear will challenge the dollar's global supremacy. To illustrate the debasement of the US dollar, today it takes $25 to buy what $1 would buy in 1913. The dollar has lost 96% of its purchasing power since 1913.

"The dollar has lost 96% of its purchasing power since 1913."

Chart 5a

The purchasing power of $1 from the time the Federal Reserve was established in 1913

1933: FDR suspends gold convertibility, makes gold illegal for U.S. citizens to own

The dollar has lost 96% of its value since 1913

1971: Nixon suspends Bretton Woods gold-exchange system

Source: BLS CPI Data

Courtesy of Zerohedge

For a longer-term view, the Minneapolis Federal Reserve provides historical Consumer Price Index (CPI) estimates from the year 1800. The CPI is an inflation indicator that measures the change in cost of a fixed basket of common products and services (otherwise known as a cost-of-living index).

Chart 5b

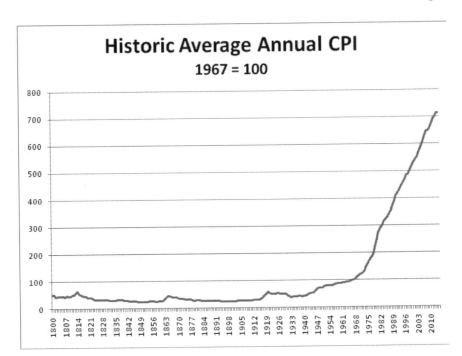

Historic Average Annual CPI
1967 = 100

Data provided by the Minneapolis Federal Reserve

Do you notice how inflation typically peaked when wars occur (War of 1812, Civil War in 1861, WWI in 1917)? Even more striking, notice the sustained inflation increase after WWII coinciding with the Bretton Woods Agreement and also in 1971 when the US severed its tie with gold.

For some, this begs the question, "Won't a crippled dollar enable another currency to reign as the global supreme currency?" Let's hope not. If the US dollar was replaced as the world's reserve currency, it would not only be economically devastating for the US, but likewise for the global economy. To try to replace the quantity of dollars in use around the world with another currency of equal or greater strength and size would thrust global commerce into a debilitating contraction and ultimately a global depression. Therefore, I believe the US dollar will reign supreme as King Dollar for our lifetime.

> ## An Example of Post-WWII Growth That Strained the Bretton Wood's Gold Standard
>
> One of the underlying themes of this book is the assumption that credit growth stimulates global economies. Under a strict gold standard, trade between countries had to balance within narrow parameters. If not, inflation or deflation would ensue, prompting a reversion to the mean. Removing the "governor effect" of a currency tied to gold enabled governments to create significant amounts of currency, as long as inflation remained tame. This has generally been the case after the US left the gold standard in 1971.*
>
> However, an astute observer would notice the continued degradation of the US dollar after Bretton Woods, despite a stated peg to gold. This is due to the US pushing the boundaries of the gold peg after WWII with a variety of global economic initiatives, such as the Marshall Plan. This plan enabled US firms to accelerate the delivery of "food and other essential products" to Europe and neighboring countries devastated by the war. A summary of the Marshall Plan helps illustrate this expansion of our trade exports. The resulting trade imbalance eventually led to excessive gold redemptions and the 1971 decision to sever the dollar peg to gold.

---

* Rampant inflation experienced by the US in the 1970s and early '80s was mitigated by a significant increase in credit growth/export expansion. This tamed inflation and led to an historic export imbalance described throughout this book.

The United States set up the European Recovery Program (known as the Marshall Plan) to provide large-scale financial and economic aid for rebuilding Europe largely through grants rather than loans. Approximately eighteen countries received financial benefits, with the largest recipient being the United Kingdom, then France. The "Axis" countries were included, with West Germany receiving the third highest amount of benefits. In a speech at Harvard University on June 5, 1947, U.S. Secretary of State George Marshall stated:

> "The breakdown of the business structure of Europe dur-ing the war was complete ... Europe's requirements for the next three or four years of foreign food and other essential products ... principally from the United States ... are so much greater than her present ability to pay that she must have sub-stantial help or face economic, social and political deteriora-tion of a very grave character."

US spending continued after the Marshall Plan, with the Korean War and the Viet Nam war adding to spending demands. Finally, social spending required by the implementation of Medicare in the mid-1960s under President Johnson was the death knell for the gold standard and the birth of today's fiat currency.

Alternatives to King Dollar

Perhaps you're not convinced the US dollar will reign supreme despite considerable headwinds. What currency could command such strength to dethrone King Dollar from the global currency title? Let's consider:

Special Drawing Rights (SDRs)
The Euro or the Yuan
Gold

Special Drawing Rights (SDRs)

The International Monetary Fund (IMF) was established by the Bretton Woods agreement to stabilize the international monetary system. SDRs were created by the IMF in 1969 as a supplemental international reserve asset due to an inadequate supply of gold and US dollars. The international community decided to create SDRs because it believed the supply of gold and dollars were inadequate to support the expansion of world trade.

According to the IMF, the SDR:

> "Is an international reserve asset, created by the IMF in 1969 to supplement its member countries' official reserves. As of March 2016, 204.1 billion SDRs (equivalent to about $285 billion) had been created and allocated to members. SDRs can be exchanged for freely usable currencies. The value of the SDR is based on a basket of five major currencies—the U.S. dollar, euro, the Chinese renminbi (RMB), the Japanese yen, and pound sterling—as of October 1, 2016."

Notice the IMF clearly states that "SDRs can be exchanged for freely usable currencies." Furthermore, "204.1 billion SDRs had been created and allocated to members." There's that money creation again! It's truly an international addiction.

The statement regarding the free exchange for usable currencies has some central bankers suggesting the SDR should replace a dollar that is declining in prestige and use around the world. True, the dollar is being sidestepped in a growing number of international transactions, but it will not be replaced by the SDR for the simple reason that there aren't nearly enough SDRs to replace the dollar.

This, however, did not deter Dr. Zhou Xiaochuan, governor of the People's Bank of China, to publish an essay titled *Reform the*

International Monetary System at the height of the Great Recession. In it, he stated:

> "The desirable goal of reforming the international monetary system, therefore, is to create an international reserve currency that is disconnected from individual nations and is able to remain stable in the long run, thus removing the inherent deficiencies caused by using credit-based national currencies." He continued, "Special consideration should be given to giving the SDR a greater role. The SDR has the features and potential to act as a super-sovereign reserve currency."

Is he right? Could the SDR replace the US dollar and act as a super-sovereign reserve currency? The exploding US Current Account deficit discussed in Chapter Two caused foreign central banks to buy dollars over the years, amassing enormous sums along the way. If the US and the world had to live under an SDR super-sovereign reserve currency standard, the global economy would literally grind to a halt in a matter of months. The US owns enough SDRs to pay China for about two months of trade. Since we cannot create additional SDRs, we would be forced to stop trading with China, or use another currency such as gold. It wouldn't take long for the US, and the world, to fall into a severe depression. Informed central bankers know this and they would never let that happen. Rest assured that talk of a global SDR standard replacing the US dollar is pure nonsense.

"If the US and the world had to live under an SDR super-sovereign reserve currency standard, the global economy would literally grind to a halt in a matter of months."

Chart 5c

Total Foreign Exchange Reserves
US$ billions, 1970 to 2014

Central banks accumulate Foreign Exchange by printing their own money and buying the currencies of other countries. Total Foreign Exchange Reserves show us how much fiat money has been created for this purpose. What we see here is an exponential explosion of fiat money creation unlike anything that had ever happened before. This was an essential element of The Dollar Standard and the global economic boom that The Dollar Standard generated.

Source: IMF

Courtesy Richard Duncan Economics

What About the Euro or Yuan?

Impossible. The currency used to replace the dollar would have to be sufficient enough to replace trillions of US dollars in circulation around the world. Furthermore, the currency would have to be trustworthy and appear free from government manipulation. While it's true the Chinese are now the world's largest producers of gold and among the top ten in gold holdings, it would take more than an attempt to peg its currency to gold to emerge as a serious global contender.

Is Gold the Answer?

I'm sorry to disappoint the gold bugs, but the answer is much like the one provided for the yuan or euro. Since the US created so many dollars and stuffed global banks as a result of our trade imbalance, the world simply does not have enough gold to replace the dollar and maintain the current level of trade. If we ever returned to a gold standard, and had to live within our means (no money creation!), the global economy would collapse.

The reason Chart 2d identified the US Current Account Balance as one of the most important economic developments of the 20th century is because this led to an explosion of global consumption the likes of which the world had never seen. The ripple effect through China, our largest trading partner, and on to countries with whom it conducts trade (such as Brazil for commodities), enhanced the lives of billions. If we do not maintain this level of growth and consumption, economies will falter. The first quarter of 2016 exemplifies the global economic reaction when countries like China slow down, taking Brazil and other dependent economies with them.

"If we ever returned to a gold standard, and had to live within our means, the global economy would collapse."

Like it or not, the world is stuck with the US dollar as our reserve currency because the amount of an alternative currency is not large enough to support global trade. Replacing the US dollar with one of these alternatives would be too painful. Like it or not, it also appears we are stuck with an addiction to QE to keep the flame of global growth flickering.

"Like it or not, the world is stuck with the US dollar as our reserve currency because the amount of an alternative currency is not large enough to support global trade."

Chapter 5 Summary

- Adherence to a gold standard helps keep inflation in check as long as governments do not allow excessive currency creation to occur.

- Since the US left the gold standard in 1971, purchasing power eroded by over 80%. A 2% inflation target may be justified, if wages keep pace with inflation. CPI moved higher after 1945 and exploded when the US decoupled from gold in 1971.

- SDRs, the euro, yuan or gold are not viable alternatives to the US dollar due to inadequate currency supplies.

- Because of the explosive growth of Total Foreign Exchange Reserves, the world is stuck with the US dollar as the world's reserve currency for the foreseeable future. It also appears we are stuck with an addiction to QE to keep the pace of global growth moving forward.

With an understanding that the US dollar will reign supreme and QE will support global asset prices, what are some of the unintended consequences from this addiction to money creation? Chapter Six will explore the detrimental effect on investors who traditionally turned to fixed-income for a reliable source of interest income.

CHAPTER **6**

QE Effect on Global
Interest Rates

*Knowledge is knowing a tomato is a fruit. Wisdom is
not putting it in a fruit salad.*

Miles Kington

I was fortunate to begin my career as a financial advisor in 1991, the beginning of a decade-long bull market. A positive stock market and generous bond yields kept most clients happy as long as I properly allocated a blend of stocks, bonds and a bit of cash to match their risk-and-return profile. Part of this portfolio typically included a bond ladder (see page 117), especially for clients in or approaching retirement. The ability to provide a steady and predictable income from bonds, perhaps 7% or more each year, was a comforting foundation from which to build their stock allocation.

Where are those badly needed 7% bond ladders today? Gobbled up by the ravages of QE, no doubt. As you recall from Chart 1b, replicated below, a desired outcome from central banks creating currency and exchanging it for government bonds is to lower bond yields. In theory, this reduces the interest rate people and corporations pay to borrow money and spurs economic development. However, lower bond yields also have detrimental consequences for retirees dependent upon higher yields for income and for pension funds seeking a stable source of cash flow.

Chart 6a

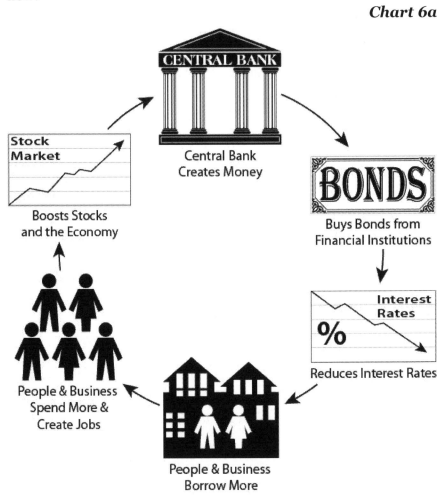

Courtesy Peregrine Associates

In addition to lowering yields, another adverse consequence to low interest rates is the tempting reach for yield by traditionally risk-adverse investors. Faced with meager yields from present-day CD rates or investment-grade bonds, investors find themselves adding dividend stocks to their portfolio, perhaps in high allotments, in order to capture an attractive yield. "And why not?" the thinking goes. Several of today's Dow blue-chip stocks sport attractive dividend yields in excess of 3%, higher than the 2% ten-year US Treasury yield. "Why not buy IBM or Proctor & Gamble stock for their rich dividend and underlying growth? What could go wrong? Stocks always go up, don't they, and the dividend is higher than the yield on many bonds."

The problem with this thinking was highlighted when stocks greeted investors in 2016 with the worst start *ever* for the Dow and S&P500 indices. All of a sudden, risk-adverse invest-ors were reminded that stocks can falter and a 3% annual dividend can be wiped out in a matter of days. Bond yields also fell, as yields typically decrease when investors sell stocks for the safety of bonds. Thank you, Fed, for another unintended consequence of your excessive QE program.

What Is a Bond Ladder?

Let's begin with the definition of a **bond**. Also referred to as "fixed-income," a bond is essentially a loan from an investor to a corporation or government. The investor lends the entity an amount of money, say $20,000, and the entity promises to repay this amount at a stated date in the future, perhaps 10, 20 or 30 years. In the meantime, since the company or government has the use of the money during this time, they pay a rate of interest each year over the life of the bond. Bond yields are affected by several variables, such as credit quality of the issuer and length of the bond term.

A bond ladder is simply a method of structuring the purchase of bonds in a systematic manner to help alleviate interest-rate risk and provide better liquidity. For example, an investor may purchase $20,000 each of bonds maturing in 5, 8, 11, 14 and 17 years. This $100,000 purchase is spread out over 12 years, providing $20,000 of available cash every three years. When the five year bond matures, the investor simply buys another bond maturing three years after the last bond, in this example the 17-year bond. If interest rates are rising, the investor locks in a higher interest rate with a portion of his assets. This strategy may be suitable for someone who does not want to purchase $100,000 of a single bond, thereby placing all his faith in one issuer, with a single interest rate over a single term, instead of a staggered term.

Speaking of Low Bond Yields ...

We've learned QE has gone global and the central bank of Japan is actually the largest owner of that nation's government bonds. If QE forces bond yields down, as Chart 6a suggests, how low have they been pushed?

Let's start with "historically low." Or, perhaps "devastatingly low" is more accurate if you are depending on them for income. In fact, government bond yields in Japan and many European countries are actually *negative*. Once again I find myself shaking my head and asking if our addiction to QE is worth the collateral damage, especially to seniors on a fixed income. Before we address the collateral damage of these low yields, here's a quick look at recent bond yields.

The Feds QE program extended the thirty-year downward trend on US Treasury bond yields. Chart 6b illustrates a continuation of falling yields, ever since we escaped the high-inflation days of the early 1980s.*

Chart 6b

Board of Governors of the Federal Reserve System (US, 10-Year Treasury Constant Maturity Rate [GS10], retrieved from FRED, Federal Reserve Bank of St. Louis https://research.stlouis-fed.org/fred2/series/GS10, May 5, 2016.

Investors waiting for US government bond yields to rise over the past several years have been sorely disappointed. To put today's low yields in perspective, yields have fallen to current levels only once before, in the mid 1940s. It's likely treasury yields will continue their descent when the Fed finally implements QE4. How low can yields fall? With the assurance of more QE, it is possible yields will eventually fall towards one-percent on the 10-year US Treasury.

---

* High inflation was tamed with the dramatic and sustained increase in consumer spending, reflected in Chart 2c (Total Credit/Debt) and Chart 2d, fall of the US Current Account Balance.

Preposterous, you say? While these would clearly be historic levels in the US, they would not be out of line from a global view. Consider what happened to the German 10-year government bond under the ECBs QE program. In April 2015 the yield fell to just seven basis points and fell to negative 17 basis points in July 2016! "Investors" purchased a 10-year German bond knowing they would not receive any interest payments during the term and at the end of 10 years, would receive less than the amount they originally paid. Amazing. Brought to you by the world's fourth largest GDP, powered by a very robust economy, under the influence of excessive QE.

What about Japan, the world's third largest economy? Spanning almost two decades, its persistent QE program has vaporized any semblance of a functioning bond market. Chapter Four informed us the BOJ owns almost 40% of Japan's government bond market. Its excessive QE program, first launched in 2001, is also responsible for driving yields on 10-year government debt to below zero percent. The BOJs announcement of a first-ever negative interest rate policy in January 2016 reveals a desperate central bank running out of policy options as it tries to breathe new life into a fragile economy.

Chart 6c

JAPAN GOVERNMENT BOND 10Y

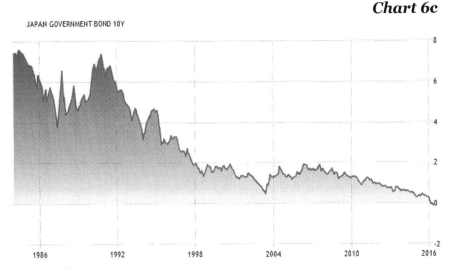

Courtesy Tradingeconomics.com

This is indeed a troubling chart, as it epitomizes a financial powerhouse in decline. We are witnessing another historic never-in-our-lifetime economic event. Japan is not a remote, isolated third-world country with little impact on the global economy. Its economy is one of the most robust in the world, ranked number three, yet it is fighting hard to make modest economic progress. Japan has the longest running QE program and, perhaps, it is beginning to understand what it means to finally run out of QE options.

Thankfully, US government bond yields are not negative or projected to fall to the lows experienced by Germany and Japan. However, this is not the case in Europe where negative rates infected 40% of the outstanding European government bonds in December 2015.

Chart 6d

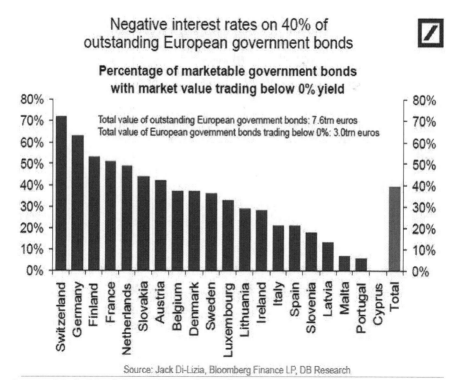

Courtesy MarketWatch, Inc. and Deutsche Bank

Are negative interest rates normal? Of course not! It's one of the main concerns surrounding the prolonged use of QE in our global economy. Excessive QE distorts normality. It's simply not prudent to overstimulate an economy well after the initial economic shock fades. Excessive QE leads to inflated stock market levels, lower bond yields and a complacent investor. If the exit from excessive QE is not properly orchestrated, innocent investors will likely experience financial pain as investment markets return to normal, pre-QE valuations. If you are not familiar with the risks associated in purchasing bonds in an extremely low interest rate environment, please read about bond basics below.

"Excessive QE distorts normality. It's simply not prudent to over stimulate an economy well after the initial economic shock fades."

Bond Basics 101

For those approaching or in retirement, it's generally prudent to allocate a portion of an investment portfolio to bonds. Typically, they represent a stable segment of a portfolio with the benefit of periodic interest payments. There are risks, however, associated with investing in "fixed-income" especially when bond yields are very low. Here's why.

It's vital to understand the direct relationship between interest rate movements (the yield a bond pays) and the value of a bond. As yields rise, the value of bonds falls. Conversely, as yields fall, the value of bonds increase.

To illustrate: Assume you purchase a $40,000 bond from IBM with a 30-year maturity that pays 5% interest. Essentially, you are lending IBM $40,000 with its promise to repay you in 30 years. While it has the use of your money during this time, it agrees to pay 5% each year in interest. What happens when interest rates rise or fall? The price of your bond will rise and fall as well. You may not be concerned about the fluctuating price if you intend to hold the bond until maturity. At the end, IBM will return your $40,000 payment and you would have earned 5% annually. However, if you want to sell your bond before maturity, you may receive more or less for the bond, depending on interest rates (all else being equal, such as the financial stability of IBM, etc.).

Fast-forward one year and assume general interest rates have risen to 6% (if IBM were issuing the same bond, it would pay 6%, not 5%). You still own your 5% bond, and have 29 years until maturity. If you want to sell this bond, it is likely you will have to accept a lower price, perhaps $35,000 for the bond, not the $40,000 you paid IBM. Why? Because investors can buy a 6% bond from IBM, making your 5% bond unattractive. To make your bond attractive, you agree to sell it for a lower price, say $35,000. The perspective buyer now sees value in buying your bond. Sure, they will only receive 5% interest payments each year for 29 years, not 6%, but they will receive a $40,000 payment from IBM in 29 years, when they only paid $35,000 to purchase the bond. The extra $5,000 payment, in their opinion, compensates for the reduced annual interest payments.

The opposite is also true. If rates decreased the first year, your 5% bond would be more valuable, since you locked in a higher rate for 29 years. If you sold this bond, you could command a higher selling price.

Pension Funding ... It's All about Cash Flow

The collateral damage of low bond yields extends beyond individual investors to the corporate world, especially pension plans. Pensions offer a promise to pay an employee a stated benefit during their retirement years. Many pensions target annual returns of 7% or more to meet current funding demands. Allocating a substantial portion of assets to bonds is normally prudent to maintain a stable investment foundation. With current yields so low, many pensions reduced their allocation to traditional bonds in favor of dividend-paying stocks or other alternative investment strategies in search of higher returns. This may be a sound investment strategy when stock prices are steadily rising, however a prolonged decline in stocks can result in immediate funding concerns.

Therefore a stock market decline such as the one that greeted 2016 can be destructive, requiring a subsequent high return to make up for losses. If not, additional contributions to the fund may be required to reach mandated funding levels. While some high profile pensions have made news for their low funding status, expect more headlines if interest rates remain historically low and a weak stock market batters investment returns. A reduced source of high, predictable cash flow from investment-quality bonds is perhaps one reason why pension fund managers are quietly cursing an over-extended QE program.

"A reduced source of high, predictable cash flow from investment-quality bonds is perhaps one reason why pension fund managers are quietly cursing an over-extended QE program."

Chapter 6 Summary

- QE drives down interest rates on fixed-income securities, such as government bonds. Many investors in or approaching retirement have relied on traditional bonds as a stable investment paying a predictable interest payment.
- With bond yields at historic lows, many investors feel forced into buying dividend stocks or other investments. Historically, these investments don't have the same stability as bonds, subjecting investors to possible portfolio fluctuations or loss of capital.
- Global bond yields have fallen to historic lows with a high percentage reaching *negative* interest rates.
- Low interest rates affect individual and professional investors alike. Many pension funds have reduced their exposure to low-yielding fixed-income investments, most likely with a corresponding increase in their investment risk profile.
- Low rates are a direct result of an excessive global QE policy. While QE was likely a prudent response to the initial financial crisis, employing its use beyond a reasonable period of time elevates the potential collateral damage for both individuals and corporations.

QE collateral damage takes many forms beyond low interest rates and elevated risk in retirement portfolios. Chapter Seven continues this discussion.

CHAPTER 7

Collateral Damage

*However beautiful the strategy, you should
occasionally look at the results.*

Sir Winston Churchill

Have you watched the first "Jurassic Park" film released in 1993? John Hammond (played by Richard Attenborough), portrays a wealthy scientist using DNA derived from fossilized mosquitoes to recreate dinosaurs on a remote island. To help convince his insurance company to underwrite the project, he hires a team of professionals to ascertain the safety and long-term viability of the extraordinary adventure park. One of these consultants is Dr. Ian Malcolm (Jeff Goldblum), a self-proclaimed "chaos expert," hired to uncover fundamental flaws that may endanger the project. Dr. Malcolm explains to a fellow traveler that chaos theory "deals with predictability in complex systems."

When Mr. Hammond is asked if the reincarnated pre-historic dinosaurs will breed in captivity, he assures the group that all dinosaurs on the island were engineered to be female, ensuring no mating will occur.

Chaos expert Dr. Malcolm is not comforted by this cavilier statement and strenuously asserts, "The kind of control you're attempting is not possible. If there's one thing the history of evolution has taught us, it's that life will not be contained. Life breaks free. It expands to new territories. It crashes through barriers. Painfully, maybe even dangerously!"

A staff scientist challenges Dr. Malcolm, asking, "You're implying a group composed entirely of female animals will breed?"

"No!" Dr. Malcolm exclaims, "I'm simply saying that *life finds a way*."

In a similar manner, perhaps the Federal Reserve and central bankers from around the world - experts in financial theory well beyond my comprehension - have found a way to tame historic financial panics, creating a tranquil landscape for investors.

Or maybe Dr. Malcolm was right, and "life will simply find a way" to prove them wrong. This chapter is devoted to several concepts that may be more powerful for even the world's most brilliant central bankers to overcome. Perhaps their best efforts are not enough to prevent financial turmoil from overwhelming markets and crashing through barriers. Painfully, maybe even dangerously.

> *"Perhaps central bank efforts are not enough to prevent financial turmoil from overwhelming markets and crashing through barriers."*

The Minsky Moment

It's a shame Dr. Malcolm and Hyman Minsky never met, as they would have enjoyed spending hours discussing the finer points of chaos theory and how it could apply to economic disruptions.

Professor Minsky (1919 – 1996) was an esteemed American economist best known for his research into the understanding and characteristics of financial crises. Famous for his development of the Minsky moment, he was a proponent of the Federal Reserve as a lender of last resort to help dampen the effects of a liquidity crisis. The definition of a Minsky moment from Wikipedia explains why this theory is gaining attention today:

> "A Minsky moment is a sudden major collapse of asset values which is part of the credit cycle or business cycle. Such moments occur because long periods of prosperity and increasing value of investments lead to increasing speculation using borrowed money. The spiraling debt incurred in financing speculative investments leads to cash flow problems for investors. The cash generated by their assets no longer is sufficient to pay off the debt they took on to acquire them. Losses on such speculative assets prompt lenders to call in their loans. This is likely to lead to a collapse of asset values. Meanwhile, the over-indebted investors are forced to sell even their less-speculative positions to make good on their loans. However, at this point no counterparty can be found to bid at the high asking prices previously quoted. This starts a major sell-off, leading to a sudden and precipitous collapse in market-clearing asset prices, a sharp drop in market liquidity, and a severe demand for cash."

The US currently enjoys "a long period of prosperity and increasing value of investments" since 2008. QE and the accompanying low interest rates have also "led to increasing speculation using borrowed money." Will cash-flow generated by the assets purchased since the Great Recession diminish, requiring over-indebted investors to sell assets in a deflationary spiral? Perhaps the presence of persistently low global interest rates is not an anomaly after all. Perhaps the prediction of rising bond yields is premature, and will only occur after the economy is cleansed by a Minsky moment?

"Since the Great Recession the global economy has been fed a steady diet of easy money fostering an increase in asset prices."

One thing is certain, since the Great Recession the global economy has been fed a steady diet of easy money fostering an increase in asset prices. Historic measures were taken to arrest an economic downturn, yet the ensuing economic rebound remains dependent upon QE. Prudent investors would do well to recognize falling bond yields as one piece of a troubling economic puzzle. Weakness in the global banking sector may be another indication of faltering asset prices. If these and other indicators point to an economic breakdown, then the preemptive QE action by central bankers is expected to continue, whether prudent or not.

Creeping Toward Deflation?

What keeps Fed governors up at night? Near the top of the list must be the fear of deflation infiltrating our economy. At a glance, deflation can be seen as a good thing, especially by consumers. Fuel prices cut in half these past two years have put a smile on the face of most consumers. Buying property at a significant discount during a Minsky moment doesn't seem like a bad deal either, at least for the buyer.

However, a general and persistent fall in prices can lead consumers to rein in spending, which can quickly put the brakes on economic growth. Perhaps consumers are waiting for prices to fall further to purchase the same item at a steeper discount. Or, they may limit their spending, preferring to keep cash in the bank during periods of instability. Regardless of the reason, a tepid US consumer is a bad sign for retailers who may curtail inventory and staff leading to an increase in unemployment, stagnant wages and exacerbating the downward spiral of prices. After all, if wages are stagnant or jobs are threatened, consumers are unlikely to continue traditional spending habits. If most consumers slow their spending, the cycle is likely to feed upon itself.

Central bankers, therefore, track the rate of inflation and potential for deflation to take prompt and decisive action before deflation becomes a threat.

The following chart is a measure of expected inflation over the five-year period that begins five years from today. The Federal Reserve finds this measure of inflation an accurate portrayal of future inflation expectations since it is less affected by cyclical factors, such as energy prices. Notice how inflation expectations have fallen since 2014. Is this a sign economic growth is in steady decline? While it is premature to believe the US economy is heading toward deflation, a persistent trend like this will clearly have the Fed's attention as it considers measures to keep a frail economy moving forward. It may be wise to take a peek at this chart a few times a year for a glimpse of what action the Fed may take to ward off any threat of deflation.

Chart 7a

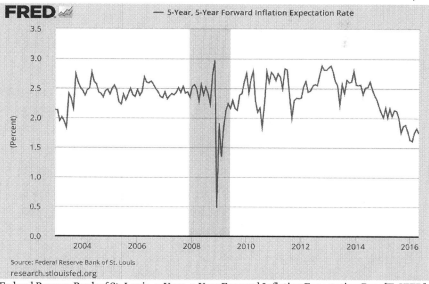

Federal Reserve Bank of St. Louis, 5-Year, 5-Year Forward Inflation Expectation Rate [T5YIFR], retrieved from FRED, Federal Reserve Bank of St. Louis https://research.stlouisfed.org/fred2/series/T5YIFR, May 4, 2016.

Unfortunately, action the Fed may take to fight deflation is what it has been doing through QE. According to Investorpedia.com,

> "Central banks often react (to deflation) by enacting a loose, or expansionary monetary policy. This includes lowering the interest rate target and pumping money into the economy through open market operations – buying treasury securities in the open market in return for newly created money. If these measures fail to stimulate demand and spur economic growth, central banks may undertake quantitative easing by purchasing more risky private assets in the open market. The central bank can also step in as lender of last resort if the financial sector is severely hindered by such events."

So, if the Fed normally fights lackluster inflation with the monetary policies described herein, and if inflation expectations are falling to levels last seen during the Great Recession, despite staggering QE efforts, is the Fed reaching the point where it is losing its ability to control our economy?

No. But it may be feeling the effect of the Law of Diminishing Marginal Returns.

The Law of Diminishing Marginal Returns

Have you ever taken a long car ride, eager to arrive at your destination? The thought of stopping for even fifteen minutes to rest seemed unthinkable. So on you drove, stopping only for gas and a quick bite to eat. At some point you grew tired, forcing you to stop for a cup of coffee. Bam! That shot of caffeine was all you needed to continue truckin' on down the road. Wide awake and alert, you felt like you could drive for hours. But then, three hours later you found yourself getting drowsy again. Time for another shot of caffeine! A second cup of coffee went down quickly and you felt good. Eyes open and your mind refocused on the destination once again. This time, however, you found yourself getting sleepy after an hour or two. No worries, as you had another cup of caffeine nearby. This time, however, it didn't give you the same boost as the first. As you reluctantly pulled over for some much needed rest, you realized the coffee jolt had stopped working.

Welcome to the Law of Diminishing Marginal Returns. As each successive cup of caffeine failed to carry the same punch as the prior dose, it eventually became ineffective - or maybe even dangerous - if it masked an underlying problem.

Global central bankers appear to be on their own journey of keeping asset prices inflated with frequent doses of QE, but asset prices are feeling the fatigue of diminishing marginal returns. Yet central bankers keep trying a variety of QE stimulants such as low or negative interest rates, government bond and mortgage security purchases, schemes like Operation Twist, numerous programs such as those outlined in Appendix One and even buying stocks in their respective stock markets! All in a quest to prevent the economy from taking a rest from its long upward journey. Is this prudent behavior?

"I firmly believe our Fed will announce QE4 and it will be a stronger dose than QE3."

Central bankers are clearly resourceful, but the frequency of their QE announcements suggests these programs are losing their effectiveness. If true, they may find the only recourse is to increase the dosage. This is one reason why I firmly believe our Fed will announce QE4, and to be effective, it will have to be a stronger dose administered for a longer period of time than QE3. No rest for the weary when it comes to stimulating stock markets! Will all the variations of QE work to guide our economy to the desired destination? What is the ultimate destination and when will central bankers finally ease off the gas pedal of perpetual QE? Answers to these questions may help ascertain if the Fed is on the right road to success, or feeling fatigued as the economy drifts off course into a ditch.

"More Bucks, Less Bang" Suggests **Bloomberg Business**

The Law of Diminishing Marginal Returns is creeping into the financial press vocabulary. Commenting on the expected increase in bond-buying by the Eurozone's central bank, *Bloomberg Business* reporter Jeanna Smialek suggested their QE efforts could deliver disappointing returns as rates are already low and cash is cheap. Specifically,

> The European Central Bank could ultimately be in for a letdown if it ramps up its mass bond-buying program in March (2016). Quantitative easing can boost the economy by pushing down interest rates that companies and households pay on loans. At its start, there was evidence that QE achieved this in the euro zone.

> But cutting rates lower at this point might have little effect in boosting economic activity: Businesses that were waiting

for low rates to borrow have probably already jumped into action, according to Carsten Brzeski, chief economist at ING-Diba in Frankfurt.

"Will corporations go out for a new loan if you cut rates from low to lower? The interest rate right now is not the issue," Brzeski said, explaining that factors like uncertainty and a lack of profitable investment options are the barriers holding investment back. "We're really at this point where more QE probably won't do any good."

Mrs. Smialek continues with comments from Ann-Katrin Petersen, vice president in global capital markets and thematic research at Allianz Global Investors. Mrs. Petersen echoes my sentiment that QE will have to be bigger and bolder to have a measurable impact on the economy. Specifically, she states, "Unless market expectations about any further stimulus delivered in March are significantly beaten, adding to purchases will probably create a less dramatic currency impact than the policy's 2015 implementation."

Sounds like the Law of Diminishing Marginal Returns in action to me.

Finally, Jennifer McKeown, senior European economist at Capital Economics provides this insightful assessment, "A diminished return is still better than no return, and I think President Draghi has made it very clear that they're not ready to throw in the towel. It needs to try to do something, and it can have some effect."

Essentially, the ECB still thinks it can motor closer to its goal with another shot of caffeine, because it is afraid to stop on its long journey and still believes more action will have "some effect."

Finally Mrs. Smialek concludes with this prescient and disturbing comment, "Policy makers may have one reason for optimism if they roll out more QE: the impact of their negative deposit rate. This might actually compound the effects of bond-buying, as the ECB noted in its January monetary policy accounts - pushing rates below zero increases market participants' incentive to get out of safe government bonds and into riskier assets."

"Riskier assets?" Is that what this is all about? Is the ultimate goal of global QE to drive investors away from safe, boring, low-yielding government bonds into riskier assets such as stocks? Will this approach ultimately save the global economy and return us to firmer financial footing? For a conservative investor, this approach may indeed prove to be quite troubling if true. As it stands, Super Mario unleashed an impressive QE package in March 2016. Even though the Fed showed its support later in the month by ratcheting back interest rate hike expectations, global markets did not show the explosive growth some expected.

"'Riskier assets?' Is that what this is all about? Is the ultimate goal of global QE to drive investors away from safe, boring, low-yielding government bonds into riskier assets such as stocks?"

End the Fed?

You can probably tell by the tone of this book that I am not a big fan of the Federal Reserve System. I believe it over-stimulated the financial markets since the Great Recession, leaving us with a severely addicted economy constantly craving the next QE fix. While the initial QE response was prudent to help stabilize a fractured economy,* subsequent stimulants have led to our current addiction, most likely making it very painful to return to normal levels.

Numerous leaders over the years have called for significant changes or the outright dissolution of the Federal Reserve. Out-spoken critic, congressman and one-time presidential candidate Ron Paul wrote a book in 2009 aptly called End the Fed to voice his displeasure with the agency. The Ludwig von Mises Institute promotes the teaching of Austrian economic theory in the tradition of Ludwig von Mises (1881 - 1973) and Murray N. Rothbard (1926 - 1995) which also vehemently opposes the existence of the Federal Reserve.

However, one outspoken critic rises above many with his call to abolish the Fed. Milton Friedman (1912 - 2006) received the 1976 Nobel Prize in Economic Science and is best known for advocating "money dropped out of a helicopter" to avoid dealing with complicated monetary policies such as those espoused by the Fed. Former Fed Chairman Benjamin Bernanke referred to Mr. Freedman's speech in 2002, forever earning him the nickname of "Helicopter Ben."

---

* Some believe it was years of poor Fed monetary policy that caused the Great Recession in the first place, however, further discussion on this possibility is outside the scope of this book.

Mr. Friedman opposed the Feds monetary policy and believed government should have a limited ability to tamper with the economy. Furthermore, he called for the abolishment of the Federal Reserve Board due to poor performance, believing a mechanical monetary system would adequately increase the quantity of money at a steady rate.

Despite increasing calls for stricter oversight, audits and scrutiny, the Fed will be with us for many years to come. Ironically, the Fed may be saved from imminent demise under the slogan "You got us into this mess, now get us out!" With our addiction to QE so severe, some argue the Fed is the only agency uniquely qualified to engineer a soft landing. Furthermore, our economy is so incredibly fragile that any serious discussion to "End the Fed" would likely lead to widespread economic chaos and stock market plunder, no matter how noble the final outcome. Like it or not, we are stuck with the Fed for now.

> *"Our economy is so incredibly fragile that any serious discussion to "End the Fed" would likely lead to widespread economic chaos and stock market plunder."*

What's Really Needed Is More Fiscal Stimulus!

As our fragile global economy finally awakens to the fact that monetary policy, otherwise known as QE, is having a diminishing effect on stimulating growth, it will ultimately turn to other revitalizing measures. Sure, we will probably have to exhaust more versions of QE, such as the purchase of stocks by our own Fed, QEs 4, 5, 6 and heightened attempts by global central bankers to lift their respective economies. But these efforts will ultimately prove tiresome, finally forcing politicians to implement *fiscal policy* measures.

Chapter Three explained the difference between monetary and fiscal policies. While monetary policies are driven by our Federal Reserve, fiscal policies derive from the US Treasury and Congress. Remember the US Treasury secretary's plea in 2008 for permission to create $700 billion to bail out troubled financial institutions? Specifically, "The US Treasury had to ask for *permission* to spend $700 billion on a bailout. Congress had to *approve* the spending and the president had to *sign* the bill into law."

If it becomes apparent that monetary policy efforts are fading and new rounds of fiscal stimulus are necessary, how do you think this news will be received by our dysfunctional Congress? Is Congress perceived as willing to work together to find common ground? Or, will it take the threat of a financial disaster for them to reach across the aisle and compromise for the good of the country?

Given the recent track record of congressional cooperation, I fear we may have to endure more stock market volatility before meaningful fiscal stimulus rides to the rescue of financial markets. As with its cousin, monetary policy, the next tranche of fiscal stimulus will have to be substantial in order to be effective. Be patient, however, as it will come. Our politicians will take their time before arriving at the right decision, but eventually they will approve a significant fiscal spending plan for the good of the country.

Okay, assuming this approach is correct, how much money is needed and what would they spend it on? Once again, I turn to economist Richard Duncan for insight he provided years ago.

Mr. Duncan anticipated the need for substantial government spending and suggested ambitious spending on momentous projects for the benefit of the US and world economies. What a concept! Specifically, when a significant government spending program is announced to revitalize a weakening US economy, why not spend $1 trillion and actually get something in return? In the aftermath of the Great Recession, the Fed created $3.6 trillion. The first trillion or so was critical as it pulled the economy from the brink of a new Great Depression. However, the only bang-for-our-buck US citizens received from the subsequent trillions in QE was inflated asset prices. For most Americans, this provided only a modest increase in 401(k) account balances or other token benefits. The true beneficiaries of excessive QE programs were those with substantial investments in stocks and other risk assets.

So what is Mr. Duncan's grand plan? He provides guidelines, but rightly leaves details to politicians who control the purse strings. In essence, his idea of getting a bang for our buck is to issue a challenge to the country (entrepreneurs large and small, corporations, university research facilities, etc.) to tackle an important problem. For example, direct the government to make $1 trillion available for research into developing the best solar panel technology the planet has ever seen.

Before I continue, let me issue an important disclaimer. This is not an endorsement for the solar panel industry! I imagine some of your faces are turning red as you shout, "That's a waste of money! Funding XYZ project would be a much better idea!" Calm down. This is only an example and one that highlights a problem inherent with this idea (further discussed below). Let's replace the words "developing the best solar panel technology the planet has ever seen" with "developing the best battery technology the planet has ever seen" or "wind turbine technology" or "nanotechnology" or "biotech research to combat disease" or ... you get the idea. Don't worry about the specific recommendation; focus on the concept that the US government makes $1 trillion available for research on a specific technology that will solve a meaningful problem with an identifiable goal. Let's get more from the next $1 trillion in fiat money creation than just ... well, just another modest increase in asset prices.

Has it been done before? Yes, and with great success! Most readers are familiar with the legendary challenge President Kennedy issued to Congress on May 25, 1961, stating, "I believe that this nation should commit itself to achieving the goal, before this decade is out, of landing a man on the moon and returning him safely to Earth." In the years that followed, the US witnessed a spirit of cooperation not seen since our great nation worked together to defeat Hitler and the Nazi's during WWII. The results of this remarkable endeavor weren't merely the success of the Apollo 11 crew, epitomized by Neil Armstrong's July 21, 1969 walk on the moon, but with the astonishing scientific advances leading up to the famous Apollo mission. Examples of these scientific innovations were recognized in 2007 on USA Today's list of the Top 25 Scientific Breakthroughs, with nine as a direct result from space exploration and eight directly from NASA programs. Furthermore, former NASA Administrator Michael Griffin explained:

> "We see the transformative effects of the Space Economy all around us through numerous technologies and life-saving capabilities. We see the Space Economy in the lives saved when advanced breast cancer screening catches tumors in time for treatment, or when a heart defibrillator restores the proper rhythm of a patient's heart....We see it when weather satellites warn us of coming hurricanes, or when satellites provide information critical to understanding our environment and the effects of climate change. We see it when we use an ATM or pay for gas at the pump with an immediate

electronic response via satellite. Technologies developed for exploring space are being used to increase crop yields and to search for good fishing regions at sea."

This is an impressive reminder of the great advancements directly attributable to NASA's space program. Being a young man in the 1960s, I'll add Space Food Sticks and Tang instant orange drink to the list!

So, can we duplicate this success today? Unfortunately, it will be very difficult. Competing agendas will likely bog down the process and limit scientific potential. Why? For the same reason I felt compelled to issue the solar panel disclaimer above. It will be very hard to find that one program where corporate interests are not infringed. Allow me to explain.

President Kennedy's challenge was in a field so new and revolutionary that no corporate interests were significantly impacted. It's not as if General Electric, IBM or General Motors had active space programs of their own to defend. A scan of the Fortune 100 companies of the time reveals most stood to benefit financially from working on the project in some fashion. There was a spirit of cooperation, especially with NASA's mandate to share technology developed during the quest. Specifically, NASA's programs states, "Technology transfer has been a mandate for NASA since the agency was established by the National Aeronautics and Space Act of 1958. The act requires that NASA provide the widest practicable and appropriate dissemination of information concerning its activities and results." Statements like this foster a spirit of cooperation and an exchange of learning for the common good.

Now back to my statement of spending $1 trillion on "developing the best battery technology the planet has ever seen." See the problem here? Do you think ExxonMobil and Chevron would be thrilled with this $1 trillion government expenditure? It's similar to funding research for a vehicle that gets 100 mpg. The funding is not likely to make the major oil companies happy, leading to years of lobbyist intervention, Political Action Committee initiatives and lawsuits to hinder the process. How about devoting $1 trillion for biotech research to combat disease? Pharmaceutical companies earn hundreds of billions of dollars selling drugs to cure the symptoms from a plethora of common ailments. Would they like the US government spending $1 trillion to find cures for some of these ailments, and in doing so limit their future revenues? Not likely. The challenge to find a common pursuit that most corporations will embrace for this $1 trillion expenditure will be daunting. I'll take the easy way out and say further discussion on this topic is outside the scope of this book. Whew.

In closing, you get the idea. At some point the effects of QE will diminish, leading to more volatility in the stock market. Since our economy is hooked on financial stimulus, the next logical source of funding will be fiscal measures to complement ongoing monetary policies. Will the fiscal measures be enough to keep our economy moving forward? Perhaps a series of smaller initiatives, easier for politicians to embrace, are more likely outcomes, such as expansive improvements to the nation's roads, bridges and tunnel infrastructure. It would help, but it's not quite as exciting as President Kennedy's epic space challenge.

Chapter 7 Summary

- Dr. Malcolm reminds us that "life will simply find a way" to disrupt even the best plans and intentions. Perhaps central bankers have found a way to soothe financial panics. Or, perhaps their best efforts are not enough to prevent financial turmoil from overwhelming markets and crashing through barriers. Painfully, maybe even dangerously.

· Professor Minsky postulates that a long period of prosperity and increasing value of investments may lead to increasing speculation using borrowed money. Ultimately a major sell off ensues, leading to a sudden and precipitous collapse in market-clearing asset prices. Has the global economy been fed a steady diet of easy money to foster an increase in asset prices? Is a Minsky moment in our future?

· Deflation fears are of utmost importance to global central bankers. Does a steady trend of falling inflation cause concern, despite their best efforts to the contrary?

· The Law of Diminishing Marginal Returns ultimately saps strength from even the most robust program. Are global economies becoming immune to the once-powerful effect of monetary policies? Brace yourself for even larger doses of QE before we come to the realization that another approach is needed.

· Calls to modify, supervise or even end the Fed intensify. However, it is likely the Fed will remain in control for years to come. Any meaningful talk of reorganization will likely send shivers through the financial markets, increasing its relevance. It got us into this mess and now it has to engineer a soft landing on the way out. Hopefully.

· When it's apparent another $1 trillion will be spent to support our economy, why not issue another epic challenge in the spirit of President Kennedy's space directive? Only politicians with fortitude and creative thinking will shepherd numerous corporate agendas toward the ideal project that aligns their special interests.

The puzzle pieces are falling into place. The final chapter summarizes information presented thus far and offers possible investments to consider.

Commentary: What Does $1 Trillion Buy?

With thanks for permission from Simon Black at www.sovereignman.com.

On October 22, 1981, the national debt in the United States of America hit $1 trillion for the first time in history.

It had taken the US federal government over 200 years to reach that mark. In that period, America had won its independence and built a nation from scratch.

We created an army and a navy, and used them both to aggressively expand the nation's domain.

We fought an incredibly bloody civil war in dispute over the most fundamental concepts of freedom.

We suffered through the Great Depression and introduced one of the most expensive public spending programs in history.

We fought two world wars and defeated the Nazis.

We developed nuclear technology. We sent people into space.

And all of that - across over 200 years of history - the USA collectively registered **one trillion dollars** in debt.

Yet despite taking two centuries to hit $1 trillion in debt, it took just a few decades to add another **$9 trillion**, growing the debt ten-fold.

On September 30, 2008 the debt crossed the $10 trillion mark for the first time. And it's never looked back since.

Now, in that 27-year period from 1981 ($1 trillion in debt) to 2008 ($10 trillion in debt), one could argue that the US had defeated the Soviet Union making the world "safe for democracy."

We waged war in the Middle East multiple times on multiple fronts.

We waged the War on Terror.

And when financial crisis struck yet again, we bailed out the US banking system.

Whether you agree or not with all of this, it's at least clear where the money went.

For the first $1 trillion in debt, there were tangible results. Independence. Defeating the Nazis. Etc. Big stuff. There was return on the investment.

For the next $9 trillion, you could at least argue that there were some actual results, like battling with the Soviet Union over the Berlin Wall or fighting global terrorism.

Now, less than eight years after hitting $10 trillion, the US government reports that it hit the **$19 trillion mark**.

What do we have to show for it?

It's not like anyone defeated the Nazis or Soviet Union over the last 8 years.

By 2008 the banks had been bailed out, and the world had supposedly been saved.

Where did all the money go? What real, tangible results do we possibly have to justify the last $9 trillion in debt?

Even more striking, compare the first trillion dollars in debt (which took 200 years to accumulate) versus the most recent trillion (which took 14 months).

What grand act took place in the last 14 months to justify another trillion dollars in debt? Nothing.

Yet in the past 14 months, both the Disability Trust Fund and the Highway Trust Fund ran out of cash.

It's extraordinary. We have reached such diminishing returns now that we can manage to squander a TRILLION dollars and have absolutely nothing to show for it.

That's the scariest part of the debt story.

It's not the total amount of the debt.

It's how quickly and easily we can fritter away $1 trillion on absolutely nothing without any trace of benefit.

It doesn't take a rocket scientist to see where this is going. In fact, even the government knows where this is going.

The Congressional Budget Office recently reported that government debt will reach $30 trillion within a decade.

Given that it took us just 9 years to rack up the last $10 trillion, that'll happen much quicker than we expect.

It's clear that this is only going to get much worse, which leaves you with essentially two options:

1) Stick your head in the sand and pretend it can go on forever without consequence;

or

2) Recognize how serious the situation is and stop the madness.

How? The answer will take more than a cursory comment with general advice.

The first step, however, is awareness of the problem. Once we admit we have a spending problem, the answer will come.

But it will take hard work, study and some of our nation's best leaders to get our country back on track. Be informed and be engaged.

The future of our great country depends on you and many more like you.

_____

Author's update:

The United States government closed out the 2016 fiscal year on September 30, 2016 with a debt level of $19,573,444,713,937.

This represents an increase of $1,422,827,047,452 over last year's fiscal year close.

In the spirit of Mr. Black's commentary, what did we "get" for this additional $1.4 trillion in debt over the past year?

In 2008, US public debt was about 64% of GDP. In 2016, it's 105%. Although the economy has grown, the debt has grown much faster.

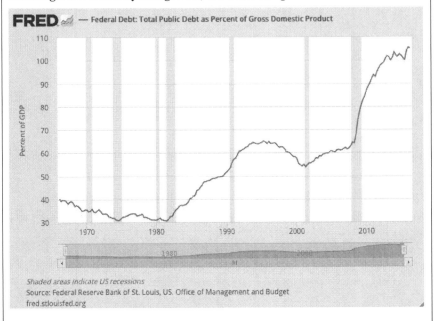

Shaded areas indicate US recessions
Source: Federal Reserve Bank of St. Louis, US. Office of Management and Budget
fred.stlouisfed.org

NASA's Gift to the World

J.R. Wilson rightfully brags about NASA's many accomplishments in his article titled "Space Program Benefits: NASA's Positive Impact on Society." Can our nation's leaders find that perfect project to provide future generations with this type of benefit? An excerpt gives us reasons to try:

"As famed heart surgeon Dr. Michael DeBakey, who has collaborated with NASA on one of its most beneficial inventions, an artificial heart pump, has said, "NASA is engaged in very active research. It has as its goal to explore space. But to do so, you've got to do all kinds of research – biological research, physical research and so on. So it's really a very, very intensive research organization. And anytime you have any type of intensive research organization or activity going on, new knowledge is going to flow from it." The story of NASA's tangible impacts on our daily lives may not garner as much attention as dramatic space missions do, but the return on investment to society from NASA's challenging activities is significant.

Courtesy of J. R. Wilson and Howard Ross, who also contributed to this article.

CHAPTER 8

How to Invest When Addicted to QE

Fall seven times, stand up eight.

Japanese Proverb

"How did you go bankrupt?" Bill asked.

"Two ways," Mike said. "Gradually and then suddenly." Ernest Hemingway's 1926 novel, *The Sun Also Rises*, reminds us that subtle warning signs may be overlooked as bankruptcy approaches. Much like the analogy of a boat drifting toward a waterfall, you may not notice the rapids until it's too late as you plummet over the edge.

While the US government, Fed and Wall Street financial systems may be treading in swift waters, I truly believe our great nation will avoid "bankruptcy" and continue down a path of slow growth until our leaders finally figure things out. Will we experience a rough ride as our economy drifts closer to the rapids? It's highly likely, and perhaps necessary, in order to recognize the change needed to get our economy back on track. The ultimate solution is best left to economists, astute politicians and leaders far more capable than me. I'm reassured knowing King Dollar will remain the supreme global currency of our planet while we find a sensible path to avoid the waterfalls ahead.

Until then, the investment landscape will be bumpy and investors should not expect the smooth ride they have taken for granted since 2009. QE acted as shock absorbers during the early years, but they are wearing out and in need of an overhaul. It will take a keen eye trained on signals from the Fed, first and foremost, followed by technical indicators and the study of promising investment sectors to carefully guide clients around the potholes of a treacherous investment landscape. Some investors may not have tolerance for the expected turbulence, seeking the safety of a gentler path instead. That may be a wise decision and is best discussed with a financial advisor whom you trust - and certainly one who understands the influence of QE on financial market.

How Should You Invest?

You now understand why this is not your father's stock market anymore. The belief that you can just buy sound investments and let them sit for years without paying attention was shattered when the Fed introduced excessive QE into the marketplace. Hopefully you now have an improved understanding of what guides our markets in this altered investment landscape and are better prepared to structure your investment portfolio. It's time to reevaluate your tolerance for risk versus your desire for growth. Then, select investments appropriate for your goals based on your new understanding of what really drives stock market performance.

So, how should you invest knowing the Fed has a chokehold over the markets? Before I provide some guidance, an important disclaimer is in order.

Obviously, investing and preserving your wealth is a serious endeavor and can be quite subjective. Providing advice to a 65 year old on the doorstep of retirement can be materially different from another 65 year old in a similar financial situation. Each may have a completely different risk tolerance, even though they both want to live off their investments in retirement. Therefore, it would be irresponsible to recommend specific strategies without a better understanding of a person's personal tolerance for risk and clear understanding of their goals. Since I am unable to do this in a book, I will not provide specific investment advice herein. Please read important information regarding this disclaimer at the end of this chapter.

For Investors Who Manage Their Own Portfolios

For those who enjoy researching the markets and directing their own portfolios, hopefully this book provided additional information to consider while you construct and manage your investments. The expectation of more QE, fiscal stimulus and global central bank activity is certain to cause further market volatility for both stocks and bonds. Whether you study technical indicators, fundamental research or other methods, I strongly suggest you stay informed about global central bank action and its effect on markets. This is not an attempt to improve your day-trading ability, but to remain well informed, and hopefully ahead of, any significant and prolonged trend in stocks, both up and down.

Remember, my simplistic rule is stock markets generally move higher with the support of QE and fall without QE. When stocks have the support of QE, increase your allocation to risk assets with a greater certainty that stocks will move higher. Without QE, a more defensive allocation would be prudent. If the knowledge you learned about QE can help protect a portion of your portfolio from another 2008 - 2009 style market drop, then it will be well worth the study and effort.

Subscribing to a macroeconomic research service such as Richard Duncan's Macro Watch would be an excellent resource for continuing your QE education. Reading about the Federal Reserve

System and coordinated central bank activity in daily news sources is also important. Appendix Three provides a few research services I found helpful. Combining these resources with systems you currently use could enhance your ability to properly manage your portfolio during the challenging times I suspect lie ahead. For the financial news junkie, I find Google Alerts of great value. I personally set alerts for "QE" and "Quantitative Easing" to allow Google to send daily news articles on these subjects. After I discard the random article about the iconic Cunard Queen Elizabeth cruise ship, I frequently find interesting articles on this important topic that help shape my overall investment strategy.

Furthermore, as you read research reports, investment articles or watch TV interviews, I suggest you carefully consider the source of the person providing the investment advice. Specifically, look for any hidden agenda the author or speaker may be hiding. Pay attention to where the expert is employed, their role in the company and experience. If Sam Smith from XYZ mutual fund company is on TV explaining why today is a great day to buy stocks, does he carry a bias because his firm sells stock mutual funds? Perhaps it's similar to visiting a car dealership and asking the salesperson if today is a good day to buy one of their cars. Of course it is, in fact, today is a great day! Therefore, scrutinize their advice to determine if it makes sense. How accurate was their previous advice? Has this person been a perennial favorite on financial TV programs frequently calling for a severe downturn in stocks? They are bound to be right sometime! Do news outlets highlight their views after turbulence rocks the market, in the hopes of better ratings?

Unfortunately, the tendency for experts to support their agenda extends to the government and Fed. On many occasions I have heard Treasury secretaries putting a rosy spin on weak economic data or Fed governors suggesting a troubling trend should be contained when the data suggests otherwise. It is a natural tendency since they see part of their role as a positive cheerleader for the economy.

When listening to expert opinions, focus on investment professionals you believe make sense, match your risk and return profile and don't support a hidden agenda. Follow the QE money trail and gauge its effectiveness on the markets. P/E ratios, company sales data and fundamental research take a back seat to the power of the Federal Reserve System. "Don't Fight the Fed" remains a prudent mantra as you ride the market swell generated from the electronic printing of trillions of dollars. And when the Fed is not feeding the printing press, reduce your exposure to risk assets such as stocks and hunker down until you have the Fed's wind at your back again.

More on Richard Duncan

In the past 25 years, I have subscribed to numerous research, advisory and technical trading services. Ever since I read Mr. Duncan's book *The New Depression: The Breakdown of the Paper Money Economy*, I have found his commentary and research of great interest. I have been a loyal Macro Watch member since he launched the program and value his insight on the growth of total credit market debt, central bank intervention in the marketplace and more. His Macro Watch program may be of benefit to financial advisors and serious investors trying to understand some of the fundamental long-term drivers of our investment markets.

As a professional courtesy, Mr. Duncan offers his Macro Watch service to my readers at a discounted annual subscription of $250.

Visit www.richardduncaneconomics.com to learn more and sub-scribe using the offer code "announcement," a synopsis of his service follows.

"When the world stopped backing money with gold in the late 1960s, our economic system changed in a fundamental way. In Macro Watch, I provide a comprehensive – and easy to understand – explanation of how it works now and what that means for the financial markets."

These courses describe how the global economy was blown into an enormous credit bubble during the decades following the breakdown of the Bretton Woods International Monetary System. They also show that, in this new era of fiat money, credit growth drives economic growth, liquidity dictates the movements of the financial markets and the government attempts to control both credit growth and liquidity to ensure that the economy does not collapse. These are the core themes that the Macro Watch videos regularly build on."

Considerations for Selecting an Appropriate Investment Advisor

For those who prefer assistance from an investment professional, you'll have to do your homework. While there are no clear guide-lines, a healthy dose of common sense will go a long way toward guiding your decision. Here are some thoughts that come to mind.

Find an advisor with passion for their work. Do they enjoy reading books on the economy and their profession? Do they study independent market research and current economic trends? Or, are they just a darn good salesperson with little understanding of how financial markets really work? One clue would be the guidance they provided during the 2016 market turbulence. Did they tell clients to just hang in there, perhaps blame market volatility on oil or an election year and offer general buy and hold advice? Or, did they explain the underlying market dynamics and ensure portfolios are allocated according to individual risk and return parameters?

"Find an advisor with passion for their work."

Is your advisor an independent thinker, or do they simply regurgitate the latest talking points from the same company strategist who spouts a frequent company refrain "our chief financial strategist says today is a great time to buy stocks because ... blah, blah, blah?"

Speaking of outdated thinking, I would personally avoid one-dimensional advisors fixated on historic performance trends: "Look at this stock market chart over the past 60 years! We expect similar results over the long term ... blah, blah, blah." Relying on these long-term historic trends was good advice during normal market environments, but a bit naive with a market under the significant influence of a QE addiction. The Fed has drastically altered the fundamentals of our investment markets and it remains to be seen what lasting effect they will have. Providing specific investment advice, especially for someone approaching or near retirement, requires interaction with an investment professional you trust before a plan can be developed and approved. This is best accomplished with someone who understands the dynamics of today's QE-enhanced markets.

If nothing else, this book has demonstrated how the Fed interfered with the stock market since 2008, altering the historic rhythm of traditional supply-and-demand dynamics. If you don't think another 2008 – 2009 style market disaster can happen again, then I believe you are mistaken. For someone near retirement, this potential for significant loss of wealth can be devastating and may permanently alter a retirement lifestyle. Perhaps you don't have the time or tolerance to sit through another 50% drop in stocks as you patiently wait (hope?) for your portfolio to recover. If this is true, make sure you work with an advisor who understands your concerns, invests accordingly and employs the proper amount of portfolio protection.

Find a consultant who takes the time to understand what is important to you. Your risk tolerance. Your return expectations. Direct them to develop a strategy incorporating a variety of investments that work together to target the growth you seek, with the protection you demand. Mistakes will be made and adjustments required, but hopefully you are working with someone who has a genuine desire to do what is best for your wallet, not theirs. In the end, both wallets should be a bit bigger if similar goals are aligned.

"Find a consultant who takes the time to understand what is important to you. Your risk tolerance. Your return expectations."

Speaking of wallets, fees will be of heightened importance if I am correct about my tepid market outlook and heightened volatility. Educate yourself about the various levels of fees, some which may be cleverly hidden. If an advisor recommends a "fee-based" investment advisory program, it may include several levels of fees, such as a program fee, investment product fee (expense ratio for a mutual fund or ETF) and the advisor fee. An advisor is entitled to fair compensation and I traditionally recommend a fee-based program for the majority of my clients. However, the fees should be reasonable for the level of service provided. Be an educated consumer and ask questions.

Is it important for your advisor to be local? Would you benefit from in-person visits on a regular basis? What firm do they represent? If you work with an investment advisor from an insurance agency, do their recommendations include an inordinate amount of insurance products? If the advisor represents a major investment firm or a bank, do you detect an over-bearing influence from the parent company (otherwise known as higher fees for little marginal benefit?). For the independent advisor, how independent are they? Do they have adequate support staff, compliance oversight and appropriate systems and procedures to ensure your personal information is protected and the companies they recommend are well-vetted and financially sound? Is it important for you to work directly with your advisor, or are they part of a large team limiting direct access to the advisor after you open an account? Does it matter if you are one client out of 200 or 2,000?

In the end, it will be up to you to clearly communicate your tolerance for risk and desire for investment return. Naturally, everyone wants strong returns with no risk, so be realistic. Some clients are eager to say they can tolerate risk when markets are rising, only to quickly call when an inevitable downturn occurs. This suggests their risk tolerance is not as high as they initially indicated. Once you finalize the risk and return parameters for your investment portfolio, perhaps some of the following investment ideas warrant consideration for a portion of a conservative portfolio knowing QE is expected to roil markets in the coming years.

Investments to Consider

As an important reminder, I am unable to provide specific investment advice in this book. What I can do, however, is describe general investment concepts you may wish to explore with your advisor if you believe the investment falls within your personal risk and return parameters. Furthermore, this is not an endorsement of my personal investment services. I urge readers to work with a local advisor who specializes in your investment objective (retirement income strategies, aggressive stock portfolios, conservative financial strategies, etc. and incorporates the previously mentioned criteria you find important.

Since I personally focus on assisting investors with conservative financial strategies, I'll discuss a few basic ideas I often discuss with clients. With volatility expected in markets as we work through our QE addiction, some of these strategies may be of interest to those who want to reduce portfolio fluctuations in exchange for modest potential returns. In no particular order, the following investments could be considered for someone in or approaching retirement with a goal of taking distributions from their portfolio while mindful of protecting the investment principle.

Large Company Dividend-Paying Stocks. Stocks are obviously a prominent investment choice with a place in most investor portfolios. Since I believe we may face turbulent markets for an extended period of time, I suggest conservative investors seeking to incorporate stocks in their portfolio consider large company stocks paying a dividend. There are factors to consider – domestic and foreign stocks, growth or value, sectors such as healthcare, utility, technology, consumer-staples and purchased in a mutual fund, ETF, annuity, UIT and other vehicles.

I favor large company domestic stocks with a record of paying a consistent dividend. If we continue to experience volatile market swings as we react to QE, oil prices, global politics and the problem du jour, these industry titans should weather the storm better than most. This is an investment category for someone with a long-term investment outlook, is attracted by the dividend yield and seeks the potential for growth if the stock appreciates in value. I typically avoid small and mid-size company stocks for retirement clients as they tend to be less stable and may not pay a consistent dividend. Remember, while the Fed has a grasp on monetary policies, slow, steady and boring may be appropriate. Diversification within large company stocks would also be advisable, perhaps using mutual funds and exchange traded funds (ETFs). If you do so, it is imperative to understand the fees, charges, expense loads and risks outlined in their prospectus and explained by your financial advisor.

Fixed-Income / Bond Investments. If you concur with my analysis that fixed income yields will remain lower for longer, then explore an appropriate allocation to traditional fixed income investments with your advisor. There are many bond sectors to consider, so select several sub-sectors that complement one another. Using mutual funds and ETFs could be appropriate to spread your investment among a variety of offerings, sectors and credit profiles. It may be wise to avoid products using "leverage." If you are not sure what leverage is, ask your advisor and understand the possible risks should we ultimately experience a sustained rising interest-rate environment. Remember to understand all the associated fees to purchase and own these investments.

Add Apartment Complexes to the Mix. For an asset class with a historically low correlation to stock movements, explore real estate. Specifically, I focus almost exclusively on apartment complexes that provide strong cash flow and properties that are well capitalized. There is a lot to understand, so work with an experienced advisor if this is a sector you wish to explore. Owner-ship comes in a variety of forms and can be purchased for as little as $10,000. In general, I currently avoid retail, office and special use real estate offerings.

Apartments top my list due to a belief rental demand and cash flow will remain strong if you invest in the appropriate type of apartment complex. Specifically, I avoid newly constructed units and prefer older buildings that have been purchased at a discount to replacement value (a good management company will seek these properties and renovate after purchase). Try to focus on properties with a history of exceptional distributions paid from ongoing operations (Funds From Operations, or FFO) and are not highly leveraged.

If you invest in a non-traded portfolio of real estate holdings (a non-traded Real Estate Investment Trust, or REIT), pay particular attention to how distributions are paid to shareholders. Insist these distributions are supported by strong cash flow. One company that merits further consideration is Resource Real Estate (www.resourcerei.com). Ask your advisor if their apartment complex REIT investments are appropriate for your portfolio.

Are You Familiar with Buy-Write or Covered-Call Option Strategies?

When some investors hear the word "options" in an investment conversation they immediately think of an aggressive trad-ing strategy. While some option strategies are aggressive, this is not the case with a covered call option strategy (also known as a buy-write strategy). This strategy is further explained below and allows you to derive additional income from stocks you currently own, while limiting the upside potential. If stocks experience a prolonged period of modest growth expectations punctuated by periods of heightened volatility, then deriving additional income from a stock portfolio while limiting gains may be prudent. Several mutual funds and ETFs incorporate a covered call strategy, or your advisor can implement this within your account, especially if you own a large single stock position. It's worth your consideration and further study.

Buy-Write or Covered-Call Option Strategies

As described by Investopedia.com:

"Widely viewed as a conservative strategy, professional investors write covered calls to increase their investment income. But individual investors can also benefit from this simple, effective option strategy by taking the time to learn it. By doing so, investors will add to their investment arsenal and give themselves more investment opportunities.

A call option is a contract that gives the buyer of the option the legal right (but not the obligation) to buy 100 shares of the underlying stock at the strike price any time before the expiration date. If the seller of the call option owns the underlying shares the option is considered "covered" because of the ability to deliver the shares without purchasing them in the open market at unknown - and possibly higher - future prices.

For the right to buy shares at a predetermined price in the future, the buyer pays the seller of the call option a premium. The premium is a cash fee paid to the seller by the buyer on the day the option is sold. It is the seller's money to keep, regardless of whether the option is exercised.

For example, let's assume you pay $50 per share for your stock and think that it will rise to $60 within one year. Also, you'd be willing to sell at $55 within six months, knowing you were giving up further upside, but making a nice short-term profit. In this scenario, selling a covered call on your stock position might be an attractive option for you.

After looking at the stock's option chain, you find a $55, six-month call option selling for $4 per share. You could sell the $55 call option against your shares, which you purchased at $50 and hoped to sell at $60 within a year. If you did this, you would obligate yourself to sell the shares at $55 within the next six months if the price rose to this amount. You would still get to keep your $4 in premiums plus the $55 from the sale of your shares, for the grand total of $59 (an 18% return) over six months.

On the other hand, if the stock falls to $40, for instance, you'll have a $10 loss on your original position. However, because you get to keep the $4 option premium from the sale of the call option, the total loss is $6 per share and not $10."

Investments That Guarantee Against Loss

Anytime you hear the word guarantee in an investment conversation, your common sense should be on alert. The guarantee is undoubtedly issued by an insurance company or through the FDIC in certain circumstances. We'll discuss insurance products, so confirm the financial strength of the insurance company first before delving into the merits of its product. Furthermore, consider these investments for a portion of your portfolio as liquidity restrictions normally apply (liquidity refers to your ability to withdraw some or all of your money from the investment during the required holding period, which is often several years). I find these investments attractive for a segment of clients interested in protecting a portion of their retirement portfolio. Similar to when we purchase insurance to protect our home against loss, buying insurance on a part of an investment portfolio may provide peace of mind and other benefit during an investment climate of heightened volatility.

The three insurance investments described below are:

- Tax-deferred fixed indexed annuities offering 100% investment protection against investment loss, modest potential for growth, strong income distribution features throughout retirement and low fees near one-percent annually.

- Tax-deferred index-linked investments with strong downside protection, potential for 6% annual growth and a zero-percent fee structure.

- Tax-deferred index-linked investments with 100% protection against loss of principle, potential for modest growth and a zero-percent fee structure.

A few comments before we proceed. The provisions discussed below will certainly change from time to time. These examples describe current investments to further explore. The common theme is a near 100% promise by the insurance company to protect your investment against loss during the holding period and low or no investment fees that erode your invested principle. The tradeoff for this downside protection and low fees structure is the expectation for lower annual investment gains and a commitment to invest for six or seven years (or a substantial penalty will be imposed).

". . . the average investor's performance over the past 20 years has significantly underperformed the overall markets by a 2.5% vs. 9.9% metric."

Why do I suggest you consider these investments? Because I believe we will experience increased volatility in financial markets, which may tempt investors to sell after experiencing losses, perhaps at the wrong time. According to a J. P. Morgan study, the average investor's performance over the past 20 years has significantly underperformed the overall markets by a 2.5% vs. 9.9% metric.* This is typically because investors sell when they can no longer bear further losses and remain on the sidelines as markets recover.

Want Lifetime Retirement Income with 99% Protection from Investment Loss?

Sounds appealing for sure, but understand the tradeoff for this protection and lifetime income. This type of protection can be

---

* J. P. Morgan. Average Investor Performance since 1995 = 2.5% while the S&P500 Index average performance since 1995 = 9.9%.

provided by a fixed indexed annuity that may incorporate some or all of the following characteristics. It is important to remember the guarantees are backed by the financial strength and claims-paying ability of the issuing insurance company. The primary reason this should be considered is for steady lifetime income. Therefore, invest with the mindset that you are giving up control of this investment for your lifetime, with the corresponding benefits it provides.

- Once your investment is accepted, it is protected 100% against loss as measured by the index you select. This is typically an annual point-to-point measurement.

- An annual fee is normally assessed, typically near one percent. Therefore, if your index loses value during a particular year, your principal is 100% protected, however the one percent fee will be assessed, decreasing your investment balance.

- A holding period for several years is common. If you decide to withdraw a substantial portion or all of your investment during this time (usually seven years), then a penalty is likely. Usually a ten-percent distribution allowance is provided each year without penalty. After the initial holding period, you are free to withdraw all of your accumulated account value without penalty. This can be more or less than your initial deposit depending on investment performance and fees.

- There are a variety of indices to consider, however I prefer a blended index of stocks and fixed-income such as the Barclays US Dynamic Balance Index II. Typically there is a spread-rate associated with this index. If this rate is

1.5%, for example, then the index will have to exceed a 1.5% increase before your investment participates in any additional gains. After this threshold, it is common to allow 100% participation in further upside movement.

· This is meant for lifetime income, so the insurance company typically guarantees a minimum amount of annual income for the rest of your life, even if the account value falls to zero. Provisions may allow for the lifetime income to extend to your spouse upon your passing. Typically a 65 year old can target a 4.5% - 5.0% distribution percentage for life.

· A unique feature of only a select number of offerings is the ability for your lifetime income to increase even after your account value falls to zero. This is a very important feature, as most annuities do not allow for further distribution increases if your account value falls below a certain threshold. Make sure you consider an investment that allows for the possibility of increasing distributions depending on the performance of your index even if your account value falls to zero.

Obviously there is much to consider, so work closely with your financial advisor to determine if this is an appropriate investment. The primary reason you should consider this is for a steady income distribution over your lifetime, or jointly if you include your spouse. Request an illustration, read the prospectus and marketing materials carefully. Ask your advisor if the Allianz Core Income 7 investment incorporates these features and is worthy of your consideration.

100% Protection Against Loss Over a Six-Year Period

Remember the good old days of 6% CD rates for a five-year holding period? Those days are long gone. However, there are alternatives that allow you to target 6% annual returns over a six year holding period with strong downside protection. Once again, an insurance company provides the guarantees, not a bank with FDIC insurance. Therefore, it is important to remember the guarantees are backed by the financial strength and claims-paying ability of the issuing insurance company. This investment may be appropriate if you want the potential of growth with guarantees against loss and no investment fees. If the following provisions are of interest to you, contact your financial advisor to learn more.

Once your investment is accepted, it is protected 100% against loss as measured by the index you select for only a portion of the loss. This is typically a point-to-point measurement over a six-year period. You select the amount of protection you prefer (I typically recommend protecting against a 25% loss).

The underlying index is usually a stock index (I prefer using the S&P500 index). Therefore, if you invest in this product with these parameters, you begin a six-year clock. At the end of the six year period, the performance of the index is calculated. If the index is positive, your investment is credited with 100% of the growth of the index up to a limit, typically 40% (representing over 6% annual growth each year).

If the index is negative over this six year period, then you are protected against loss up to a certain percentage (in this example, 25%). So, if the S&P500 index fell 25% during your six-year holding period, 100% of your investment would be returned. Any loss greater than 25% would reduce the value of your investment. For example, if the index lost 30% over six years, you would lose 5% of your investment.

There is no annual fee or any spread-rate assessed, therefore fees do not decrease the value of your investment during this time.

A holding period for six years is common. If you decide to withdraw a substantial portion or all of your investment during this time, then a penalty is likely. Usually a 10% distribution allowance is provided each year without penalty. After the initial holding period you are free to withdraw all of your accumulated account value without penalty.

There are several indices to consider, however I prefer the S&P500 index since it represents a broad range of large stocks.

This is not meant for lifetime income and is typically used as an investment providing the potential for growth with protection against loss over a finite period of years.

The primary reason you should consider this is for growth potential over several years with significant protection against loss. Request an illustration, read the prospectus and marketing materials carefully as subsequent rates and features are likely to change. Ask your advisor if the MetLife Shield 25 investment incorporates these features and is worthy of your consideration.

Diversify Your 100% Protection Against Loss Over a Six-Year Period

If we return to negative annual returns and volatility in the stock market, then it may be prudent to get creative with your investments. Unfortunately, this is likely a result of global central bank ZIRP and NIRP (Negative Interest Rate Policy).

Consider a variation of the six-year point-to-point investment described above with a similar investment incorporating an annual or two-year point-to-point measurement. An insurance company provides the guarantees, not a bank with FDIC insurance. Therefore, it is important to remember the guarantees are backed by the financial strength and claims-paying ability of the issuing insurance company. This investment is also appropriate if you want the potential of growth with guarantees against loss and no investment fees. If the following provisions are of interest to you, contact your financial advisor to learn more.

- Once your investment is accepted, it is protected 100%against loss, even if the underlying index falls fifty-percent or more.
- To diversify your potential investment returns, I recommend using an annual guaranteed return and two additional crediting methods using the S&P500 index. Invest one-third of your capital in an annual guaranteed account, currently offering a 2% rate, one-third in the S&P500 index currently offering the potential for 3.35% annual growth and one-third in the S&P500 index currently offering nearly 8% potential growth over a two-year period.
- The 2% rate is easy to explain. Regardless of how financial markets perform, one-third of your investment is credited with 2% during the first year and this rate may adjust with interest rates in subsequent one-year periods. With the 10-year US Treasury Note currently yielding less than 2%, this is an attractive rate. For one-third of your investment, use the annual S&P500 "performance-triggered" account, currently near 3.35%. If, during the one-year period, the performance of the S&P500 index is 0.0% or higher, your investment is credited with 3.35% growth. If the index is 1%, you earn 3.35%.

If it is 10%, you earn 3.35%. If it loses value during the year, you receive no credit and are protected 100% against loss. For the remaining one-third, invest in a two-year point to point using the S&P500 index for measurement and a current 7.95% maximum growth potential. This method uses the actual performance of the S&P500 for the crediting method. If the index is up 4% over two years, you have 4% credited to your account. A 12% return earns you a 7.95% credit. A loss of any amount preserves 100% of your account value.

- There is no annual fee or any spread-rate assessed, therefore fees do not decrease the value of your investment during this time.

- A holding period for six years is common. If you decide to withdraw a substantial portion or all of your investment during this time, then a penalty is likely. Usually a 10%distribution allowance is provided each year without penalty. After the initial holding period you are free to withdraw all of your accumulated account value without penalty.

- There are several indices to consider, however I prefer the S&P500 index since it represents a broad range of large stocks.

- This is not meant for lifetime income and is typically used as an investment providing the potential for growth with protection against loss over a finite period of years.

The primary reason you should consider this investment is for growth potential over several years with 100% protection against loss. Request an illustration, read the prospectus and marketing materials carefully as subsequent rates and features are likely to change. Ask your advisor if the Lincoln Financial Group - New Directions investment incorporates these features and is worthy of your consideration.

Are Low-Cost Professionally Managed Accounts Best for You?

If you are a long-term investor interested in targeting index-like returns with professional management and relatively low fees, there are a few programs to consider. If I am correct, investors should expect lower investment returns in the coming years and ensure the fees charged to manage your accounts are reasonable.

As a reminder, an investment account managed by your advisor or an investment program within their firm may have several layers of fees. They may include a program fee, compensation to the advisor for monitoring the account and the fee for the underlying investments (mutual funds, ETFs, etc.).

A program fee is often charged to pay for the management team that constructs and monitors the overall program. If you use a program offered by a large investment firm within a bank, for example, it is likely they charge a nominal fee to pay for the team that manages this program, provides the reporting, pays for transaction charges when investments are bought and sold, etc. If mutual funds or ETFs are used within the program, each of them has individual fees. Finally, your investment advisor is entitled to a fee to manage the overall program, notify you of important changes and suggest improvements when necessary. All of these fees may add up to 2% - 3% of your account value (for example, a program fee of 0.25%, mutual fund fees of 1.0% and an advisor fee of 1.2%). This may be an aggressive fee structure if we remain in a slow growth environment.

If the diversification in your portfolio calls for investing in an array of traditional stocks and bonds for the long term, then consider one of several large independent investment firms to reduce expenses while combining professional management. I will use the SEI investment firm located in Oaks, PA (www.seic.com) as an example of a company I recommend for this purpose. Be sure to ask your investment advisor about this or similar companies they recommend.

For me, SEI combines professional investment management with low fees for solid long term investment results. I do not expect their investments to hit periodic "home-runs," nor do I anticipate significant downside investment surprises. If they deliver steady returns near their benchmark with average or below average fees, I am pleased. For this, my clients receive an investment policy statement, professional monitoring of investments and reasonable fees from a company that manages or administers over $670 billion in assets. Because of their size and structure, a recent proposal for a $400,000 account in a 60% bond and 40% stock allocated portfolio generated a total fee of 1.55% to the client (includes program fee, fund fees and advisor compensation). I find this to be reasonable for the quality service they provide. If this type of investment program is of interest to you, ask your advisor for a recommendation on this or a similar investment program. As always, investigate the financial strength, history, integrity, performance, terms and conditions of the company you select. There are many variables to consider and a qualified investment advisor is instrumental in assisting with your ultimate selection.

Are you Concerned about Excessive Medical Bills in Retirement?

Some retirees worry that dementia or other debilitating diseases may require extensive and costly medical attention at some point during retirement. If this is a concern, discuss options with your financial advisor and consider a Long Term Care (LTC) insurance policy to help defray these costs and preserve a portion of your retirement assets. Although this investment has little to do with investing in a QE enhanced market, it is a prudent discussion for those approaching retirement to protect and diversify assets.

There are several ways to purchase LTC, such as a stand-alone policy, within an annuity and LTC included in a life insurance policy. While each situation is unique, I generally explore an LTC rider with a life insurance policy for most clients and avoid a stand-alone LTC policy. In some circumstances, I may consider an annuity with an LTC option. Furthermore, I typically prefer a universal-life policy, not a whole-life policy, to keep premiums low with a focus on pure insurance and less "built-up cash value" within the policy. Situations are unique, so explore the appropriate approach with your advisor if this type of protection is important.

A typical universal-life insurance policy with LTC rider normally allows your premium payment to cover one of three possibilities. A 62 year old female in good health, for example, may pay $5,000 per year for a $250,000 policy that provides one of the three possible outcomes:

- No long term care is needed during retirement and the beneficiaries receive a $250,000 death benefit upon passing.
- Extended long term care is needed and the policy distributes the entire $250,000 over the course of several years. A typical policy will limit distributions to $5,000 per month until the $250,000 is reached. The policy then terminates and no death benefit or further payments are expected.
- Long term care is needed, however only a portion of the $250,000 is paid in LTC benefits, with the remaining

balance paid as a death benefit. For example, if $100,000 in LTC benefits are paid prior to passing, then the beneficiaries receive a $150,000 death benefit.

These examples demonstrate how a single premium payment allows for multiple distributions. In all examples, the premium payment provides some level of benefit. Make sure the policy pays benefits once the owner is unable to perform two of six Activities of Daily Living (ADLs) as verified by their physician. Payments should be paid upon request without proof of expense receipts and should cover home health care, nursing home care, assisted living care and adult day care. The payments should be payable to the policy owner, allowing them to pay a friend or relative for their assistance, for example, even though they may not be a licensed health care professional. It is important to work with a financially strong and reputable company, and an advisor with experience with these policies.

Let's Wrap It Up!

You undoubtedly have a much better understanding of what is currently driving global financial markets. Every time you read or hear about central bank activity, look for a corresponding reaction in stocks, bonds and currencies. Was the stimulus large enough to cause a prolonged move higher? Or, is the Law of Diminishing Marginal Returns tamping down QE expectations and pointing toward fiscal measures to provide the economic stability governments seek?

As a reminder, here are some of the macro themes to follow as financial markets try to find their footing along a precarious path:

- When QE4 is announced by our Fed, ensure that it is a substantial effort (as big or bigger than QE3) before you

increase exposure to risk assets. When the Fed announces
or is suspected of buying stocks in our stock market, it will
also be time to increase exposure to stocks.

. Don't fight the Fed! However, be wary of its reduced
impact on stimulating the markets. As the Fed gets desperate, it will try bigger and bolder initiatives. The Fed can act
quickly and decisively, whereas fiscal policy must shuffle
its way through a lengthy approval process. A divided Congress will only belabor the process.

. Interest rates will continue lower for longer. Avoiding
deflation will remain a high priority and hidden objective
for the Fed. When the Fed highlights its ambition to target
a modest two-percent inflation rate, it is actually
confirming a concern about deflation. Fed officials will
take drastic measures to avoid deflation. Global
government bond yields will continue to fall as ZIRP and
NIRP become commonplace, with a one-percent yield on
the US 10-Yr Treasury a likely target. Watch yields on
global 10-year government bonds from Japan, Germany,
UK, Spain, Italy and other major markets for a clue on
the overall trend.

. Without admitting to a failure of its December 2015 rate
hike, the Fed will find a reason to stop increasing the Fed
funds rate and will actually lower it to effectively zero once
again. NIRP will be discussed, but implementing this policy
will take time.

. The US stock market will remain choppy with a downward
bias until substantial liquidity re-enters the marketplace.
Global central bankers will remain in close contact as they
coordinate their response. At some point, pressure will
mount for dedicated fiscal stimulus, generating howls from

fiscal conservatives and fist-pounding demands for action by high-profile economists. The correct answer will be elusive, however a spending plan such as the one suggested by Mr. Duncan in Chapter Seven should receive meaningful attention. Another approach he suggests is for the government to finance a significant fiscal spending program and have the Fed create enough currency to purchase the newly issued government bonds. Unfortunately, many obstacles must be overcome before a prudent policy can be reached.

"If we return to a Wall Street and Washington government that are respectful of our middle class and the values that made our country great, there will always be hope for better days."

More than anything, my advice is to have faith in American citizens and politicians to find the right approach. It may take time, and we may have to endure pain, however, we will likely be stronger for the process. I love our country and served proudly in the USMC for many years. Although I am disappointed in decisions made by the Fed and our government since the Great Recession, hindsight is always 20/20. If we return to a Wall Street and Washington government that are respectful of our middle class and the values that made our country great, there will always be hope for better days.

Important Disclosure Regarding Information Provided Herein

The information contained herein are solely my opinions and do not necessarily represent the view of firms associated with my profession, including, but not limited to, Doylestown Wealth Management, LPL Financial, Great Valley Advisor Group or affiliates. Opinions expressed herein are statements of my judgment as of the publication date and are subject to change without notice. This information is issued solely for informational purposes and does not constitute an offer to sell or a solicitation of an offer to buy securities. Past performance is not a guarantee, nor is it necessarily indicative, of future results. This information is not meant as tax or legal advice. You should consult with the appropriate tax or legal professional before making investment decisions. Information contained herein is based on sources that I believe to be reliable but is not guaranteed by me as being accurate and does not purport to be a complete statement or summary of available data. When evaluating investments, carefully consider all fees, charges and expenses and read the prospectus for complete information. Terms and conditions of investments discussed herein are expected to change, therefore, it is important to evaluate current investment parameters before arriving at a decision. Consult with a qualified financial professional before investing to ensure you are taking action that is appropriate for your personal risk tolerance and desire for investment growth.

Appendix One

Emergency Funding Programs Established by the Federal Reserve System and US Treasury Department During the Great Recession of 2007 – 2009

During the financial crisis of 2008-2009, the Federal Reserve System and US Treasury Department implemented several emergency funding programs to rescue firms in distress. The following synopsis illustrates the magnitude of the economic duress, which required historic remedies to save our economy from financial failure. As you read through the list, the Fed, the Treasury and our economy faced one financial challenge after another, calling for extreme measures and unique solutions. For some, the financial panic of 2008-2009 is a distant memory, locked away under the category of "That will never happen again." However, history has a habit of repeating itself, or at least it rhymes. Therefore, it may be wise to refresh our memory of the panic that many of our largest companies endured and the Fed's response.

Pay particular attention to time frames, as it is remarkable that once venerable financial firms were reduced to bankruptcy in a matter of months. Take Bear Stearns for example. According to Wikipedia, the company employed 15,500 people worldwide in 2007. In 2005–2007, Bear Stearns was recognized as the "Most Admired" securities firm in Fortune's "America's Most Admired Companies" survey. This was the second time in three years Bear Stearns had achieved this top distinction. As a result of this recognition and strong earnings reports, their stock price closed at an all-time high of $171.51 on January 12, 2007. It wouldn't take long for their excessive bet on shaky subprime mortgage investments to crater the stock, as it fell 99% over the next 14 months when JP Morgan finally agreed on March 16, 2008 to buy the company for $2/share.

Is it prudent for the Fed and our government to rescue firms in financial distress such as Bear Stearns, AIG, GM etc., or should the market determine a fair price and punish them for poor judgment and excessive risk-taking? Does a Fed bailout foster a sense of comfort within large companies, knowing the Fed can step in to rescue creditors of bankrupt firms – such as payments made to Goldman Sachs when AIG failed or Merrill Lynch when it "merged" with Bank of America? Time will tell if the Fed will have to resurrect some of these programs or conjure new treatments next time a large company faces a financial disaster. I believe it's a matter of when, not if.

The following is a synopsis of initiatives the Fed and US Treasury took to help restore faith in the US economy as described on the Federal Reserve website.

Reading from the Fed's website,

"During the financial crisis, the Federal Reserve established several facilities to provide liquidity directly to borrowers and investors in key credit markets. As the performance of financial markets has improved, the Federal Reserve has wound down some of the programs."

The liquidity provided for many of these programs is reflected in Chart 2g "All Federal Reserve Banks – Total Assets, Eliminations from Consolidation." As you know, the totals reached several trillion dollars and the balance sheet remains elevated at this level today.

We begin with a summary of the Treasury's Troubled Asset Relief Program (TARP) and conclude with a description of several emergency initiatives undertaken by the Fed.

Troubled Asset Relief Program (TARP)

· October 8, 2008, Fed Commits Additional $37.8 Billion to AIG

The Federal Reserve announces that the Federal Reserve Bank of New York (FRBNY) will borrow up to $37.8 billion in investment-grade, fixed-income securities from AIG in return for cash collateral. This support is in addition to the previous $85 billion credit facility the Fed provided to AIG – and will bring the Fed's overall commitment to AIG to a total of nearly $123 billion. On November 1, 2008, Treasury invested another $40 billion in senior preferred stock of AIG.

· October 13, 2008, GM CEO Requests Up to $10 Billion

GM CEO Rick Wagoner met with Secretary Paulson and requested a $5 billion loan and $5 billion line of credit to stave off a bank-like run from the company's creditors and suppliers.

· October 14, 2008, $125 Billion Committed to Nine Large Financial Institutions

Treasury, the Federal Reserve, the FDIC, and OCC jointly announced the launch of the Capital Purchase Program (CPP) under TARP to inject up to $250 billion in banks. Nine large financial institutions have already signed on to receive $125 billion through the program. Treasury purchased $25 billion in preferred stock from Citigroup under the CPP.

. November 10, 2008, Fannie Reports $29 Billion Loss
Fannie Mae reported a $29.0 billion net loss for the third quarter
of 2008, reducing its net worth to $9.0 billion. Fannie also states
that "If current trends in the housing and financial markets continue or worsen, and we have a significant net loss in the fourth
quarter of 2008, we may have a negative net worth as of December 31, 2008 . . . [and] would be required to obtain funding from
Treasury."

. November 14, 2008, Mayors Request TARP Funds
The mayors of three large cities – Philadelphia, Phoenix, and
Atlanta – sent a letter to Secretary Paulson requesting $50 billion
in TARP funds to help their cities deal with financial obligations.

. November 23, 2008. Government Announces Additional Assistance for Citi
Treasury, the Federal Reserve, and the FDIC announced an agreement to provide further aid to Citigroup. Under the agreement, the
government would insure a pool of $306 billion in assets against
unusually large losses. Citigroup would have responsibility for the
first $29 billion in losses. Any losses in excess of that amount would
be shared between the government (90%) and Citigroup (10%).
The government's share of those losses would first be allocated to
Treasury through TARP (up to $5 billion); second to the FDIC (up
to $10 billion); and the remainder through a non-recourse loan
from the Federal Reserve. Treasury also agrees to invest an additional $20 billion in Citigroup from TARP in exchange for pre-
ferred stock with an eight percent dividend to the Treasury. In
addition to the higher dividend rate than available through the
Capital Purchase Program (CPP), Citigroup would be required to
comply with enhanced executive compensation restrictions and to

implement the FDIC's mortgage modification program as a part of this investment.

• December 2, 2008, Big Three Automakers Request $34 Billion

The Big Three automakers submitted restructuring plans to Congress requesting a combined $34 billion in loans and lines of credit – $18 billion for GM, $7 billion for Chrysler, and $9 billion for Ford. Ford stated that it does not immediately need a loan, but requested a line of credit in the event that economic and auto industry conditions deteriorate further. On 12/19/08, the Bush Administration agreed to provide $17.4 billion in loans to GM ($13.4 billion) and Chrysler ($4.0 billion) through TARP. On 12/29/08, Treasury announced that it will purchase $5 billion in preferred stock from GMAC, and loan up to $1 billion to GM to purchase additional equity in GMAC. Under this agreement, Treasury has the ability to exchange its $1 billion loan to GM for the GMAC equity GM purchased with that loan.

• December 19, 2008, Paulson Announces First $350 Billion in TARP Funds Fully Allocated

After committing funds to the auto industry, Secretary Paulson announced that "Treasury effectively has allocated the first $350 billion from the TARP...It is clear, however, that Congress will need to release the remainder of the TARP to support financial market stability. I will discuss that process with the congressional leadership and the president-elect's transition team in the near future."

(Author's note, this effectively ends TARP funding, as the new Obama administration will dictate their financial response and priorities.)

The Federal Reserve System website provides the following synopsis of its funding efforts.

Bear Stearns, JPMorgan Chase and Maiden Lane LLC #1

In March 2008, The Bear Stearns Companies, Inc. was one of the largest securities firms in the country, with reported total consolidated assets of nearly $400 billion. Bear Stearns engaged in a broad range of activities, including investment banking, securities and derivatives trading and clearing, brokerage services, and originating and securitizing commercial and residential mortgage loans. Financial conditions for the firm deteriorated markedly between mid-January and mid-March 2008. On March 13, 2008, Bear Stearns notified the Federal Reserve that it expected that it would not have enough funding or liquid assets to meet its financial obligations the following day and would not be able to find a private-sector source of alternative financing.

The imminent insolvency of Bear Stearns, the large presence of Bear Stearns in several important financial markets (including, in particular, the markets for repo-style transactions, over-the-counter derivative and foreign exchange transactions, mortgage-backed securities, and securities clearing services), and the potential for contagion to similarly situated firms raised significant concern that the stability of financial markets would be seriously disrupted if Bear Stearns were suddenly unable to meet its obligations to counterparties, and the extension of credit allowed for an orderly resolution of the firm.

To address the immediate liquidity needs of Bear Stearns and forestall the potential systemic disruptions that a default or bankruptcy of the company would have caused in the already stressed credit markets, on Friday, March 14, 2008, the Federal Reserve Board authorized the Federal Reserve Bank of New York (FRBNY) to extend credit to Bear Stearns through JPMorgan Chase Bank, N.A. (JPMC Bank). The purpose of this bridge loan was to ensure that Bear Stearns would meet its obligations as they came due that day, allowing for time during the weekend for Bear Stearns to explore options with other financial institutions that might enable it to avoid bankruptcy and for policymakers to continue to seek ways to contain the risk to financial markets in the event no private-sector solution proved possible. The loan to Bear Stearns was in the amount of $12.9 billion and was secured by assets of Bear Stearns with a value of $13.8 billion. The FRBNY received no warrants or any other potential equity of either JPMC Bank or Bear Stearns in exchange for the loan, and the loan was made without recourse to JPMC Bank. On the morning of Monday, March 17, the $12.9 billion was repaid in full to the FRBNY with interest of nearly $4 million.

The bridge loan was extended under the authority of Section 13(3) of the Federal Reserve Act, which permitted the Board, in unusual and exigent circumstances, to authorize Reserve Banks to extend credit to individuals, partnerships, and corporations.

Maiden Lane LLC #1

Despite the receipt by Bear Stearns of Federal Reserve funding through a bridge loan on March 14, 2008, market pressures on Bear Stearns worsened that day and during the weekend. Bear Stearns likely would have been unable to avoid bankruptcy on Monday, March 17, without either very large injections of liquidity from the Federal Reserve or an acquisition by a stronger firm. JPMorgan Chase and Co. (JPMC) emerged as the only viable bidder for Bear

Stearns, and on Sunday, March 16, Bear Stearns accepted an offer to merge with JPMC.

However, JPMC was concerned about its ability to absorb a portion of Bear Stearn's mortgage trading portfolio, given the uncertainty about the scale of potential losses facing the financial system at the time and strained credit markets.

To facilitate a prompt acquisition of Bear Stearns by JPMC, the FRBNY created a limited liability company, Maiden Lane LLC, to acquire that set of assets of Bear Stearns. The FRBNY extended credit to the LLC, which would then manage those assets through time to maximize the repayment of credit extended to the LLC and to minimize disruption to financial markets. Maiden Lane LLC purchased approximately $30 billion in assets from Bear Stearns with a loan of approximately $29 billion from the FRBNY. Under the terms of the agreement, JPMC also lent roughly $1 billion to Maiden Lane in a loan that is subordinated to the loan from the FRBNY for repayment purposes (according to the FRBNY, on June 14, 2012, ML LLC repaid the loan made by the New York Fed, with interest).

American International Group (AIG, Maiden Lane II and III

AIG was a large, diversified financial services company that, as of June 30, 2008, reported consolidated total assets of slightly more than $1 trillion. During the months prior to September 2008, short-term funding markets had come under severe stress, placing significant liquidity pressures on AIG that hindered its ability to obtain adequate funding from banking institutions or in the market, and threatened to prompt a default by the firm (Authors note: AIGs stock price fell from a split-adjusted price of $1,453 in June 2007 to $34 in October 2008.)

The potential failure of AIG during the financial crisis posed significant systemic risks: AIG's insurance subsidiaries were among the largest in the United States; state and local governments that had lent money to AIG might have suffered losses; retirement plans had purchased insurance from AIG; banks and insurance banks had large exposures to AIG; a default by AIG on its commercial paper likely would have disrupted the entire commercial paper market. These potential disruptions to financial markets and losses by other major financial institutions, at a time when the financial system was already under severe stress, likely would have resulted in a significant further reduction in the availability of credit to businesses and households, worsening the recession.

On September 16, 2008, the Federal Reserve announced that it would lend to AIG to provide the company with the time and flexibility to execute a plan that would allow it to restructure to maximize its value. Initially, the FRBNY extended a line of credit to AIG for up to $85 billion. The revolving credit facility was established to assist AIG in meeting its obligations as they came due and to facilitate a process under which AIG would sell certain of its businesses in an orderly manner, with the least possible disruption to the overall economy.

On November 10, 2008, the Federal Reserve and the Treasury announced a restructuring of the government's financial support to AIG. As part of this restructuring, two new limited liability companies (LLCs), Maiden Lane II LLC and Maiden Lane III LLC, were created. On December 12, 2008, the FRBNY began extending credit to Maiden Lane II LLC, which was formed to purchase residential mortgage-backed security (RMBS) assets from AIG subsidiaries. Details of the terms of the loan are published on the FRBNY website Leaving the Board. Maiden Lane II LLC was funded with a $19.5 billion senior loan from the FRBNY and $1 billion from

AIG through a contingent purchase price adjustment. The loan extended by the FRBNY is collateralized by the asset portfolio.

On November 25, 2008, the FRBNY began extending credit to Maiden Lane III LLC, a limited liability company formed to purchase multi-sector collateralized debt obligations (CDOs) on which AIG had written credit default swap and similar contracts in return for the cancellation of those contracts. Details of the terms of the loan were published on the FRBNY website Leaving the Board. Maiden Lane III LLC was funded with a $24.3 billion senior loan from the FRBNY and a $5 billion equity contribution from AIG.

Money Market Investor Funding Facility (MMIFF)

The Money Market Investor Funding Facility was designed to provide liquidity to U.S. money market investors. Under the MMIFF, the Federal Reserve Bank of New York could provide senior secured funding to a series of special purpose vehicles to facilitate an industry-supported private-sector initiative to finance the purchase of eligible assets from eligible investors. The MMIFF was announced on October 21, 2008, and expired on October 30, 2009.

Asset-Backed Commercial Paper Money Market Mutual Fund Liquidity Facility (AMLF)

The Asset-Backed Commercial Paper Money Market Mutual Fund Liquidity Facility was a lending facility that provided funding to U.S. depository institutions and bank holding companies to finance their purchases of high-quality asset-backed commercial paper (ABCP) from money market mutual funds under certain conditions. The program was intended to assist money funds that held such paper in meeting demands for redemptions by investors and to foster liquidity in the ABCP market and money markets more generally. The AMLF began operations on September 22, 2008, and was closed on February 1, 2010.

Commercial Paper Funding Facility (CPFF)

The Federal Reserve created the Commercial Paper Funding Facility (CPFF) to provide a liquidity backstop to U.S. issuers of commercial paper. The CPFF was intended to improve liquidity in short-term funding markets and thereby contribute to greater availability of credit for businesses and households. Under the CPFF, the Federal Reserve Bank of New York financed the purchase of highly rated unsecured and asset-backed commercial paper from eligible issuers via eligible primary dealers. The CPFF began operations on October 27, 2008, and was closed on February 1, 2010.

Primary Dealer Credit Facility (PDCF)

The Primary Dealer Credit Facility was an overnight loan facility that provided funding to primary dealers in exchange for a specified range of eligible collateral and was intended to foster the functioning of financial markets more generally. The PDCF began operations on March 17, 2008, and was closed on February 1, 2010.

Term Securities Lending Facility (TSLF)

The Term Securities Lending Facility was a weekly loan facility that promoted liquidity in Treasury and other collateral markets and thus fostered the functioning of financial markets more generally. The program offered Treasury securities held by the System Open Market Account (SOMA) for loan over a one-month term against other program-eligible general collateral. Securities loans were awarded to primary dealers based on a competitive single-price auction. The TSLF was announced on March 11, 2008, and the first auction was conducted on March 27, 2008. The TSLF was closed on February 1, 2010.

Term Auction Facility (TAF)

Under the Term Auction Facility, the Federal Reserve auctioned term funds to depository institutions. All depository institutions that were eligible to borrow under the primary credit program were eligible to participate in TAF auctions. All advances were fully collateralized. Each TAF auction was for a fixed amount, with the rate determined by the auction process (subject to a minimum bid rate). Bids were submitted by phone through local Reserve Banks. The fi al Term Auction Facility auction was conducted on March 8, 2010.

Term Asset-Backed Securities Loan Facility (TALF)

The Term Asset-Backed Securities Loan Facility was a funding facility that helped market participants meet the credit needs of households and small businesses by supporting the issuance of asset-backed securities (ABS) collateralized by loans of various types to consumers and businesses of all sizes. Under the TALF, the Federal Reserve Bank of New York (FRBNY) loaned up to $200 billion on a non-recourse basis to holders of certain AAA-rated ABS backed by newly and recently originated consumer and small business loans. The FRBNY extended loans in an amount equal to the market value of the ABS less a haircut and these loans were secured at all times by the ABS. The US Treasury Department--under the Troubled Assets Relief Program (TARP) of the Emergency Economic Stabilization Act of 2008--provided $20 billion of credit protection to the FRBNY in connection with the TALF. The TALF began operation in March 2009 and was closed for new loan extensions on June 30, 2010. The final outstanding TALF loan was repaid in full in October 2014.

Maturity Extension Program and Reinvestment Policy (*AKA, Operation Twist*)

Under the maturity extension program, the Federal Reserve sold or redeemed a total of $667 billion of shorter-term Treasury securities and used the proceeds to buy longer-term Treasury securities, thereby extending the average maturity of the securities in the Federal Reserve's portfolio. By putting downward pressure on longer-term interest rates, the maturity extension program was intended to contribute to a broad easing in financial market conditions and provide support for the economic recovery. The Federal Open Market Committee (FOMC) announced a $400 billion program in September 2011 that was to be completed by the end of June 2012. In June 2012, the FOMC continued the program through the end of 2012, resulting in the purchase, as well as the sale and redemption, of an additional $267 billion in Treasury securities.

Agency Mortgage-Backed Securities (MBS) Purchase Program

In response to the emerging financial crisis, and in order to mitigate its implications for the US economy and financial system, the Federal Reserve eased the stance of monetary policy aggressively throughout 2008 by reducing the target for the federal funds rate. By December of 2008, the Federal Open Market Committee (FOMC) had reduced its target federal funds rate to a range of between 0 and 1/4 percent. With the target federal funds rate at the effective lower bound, the FOMC sought to provide additional policy stimulus by expanding the holdings of longer term securities in its portfolio, the System Open Market Account (SOMA), including large-scale purchases of fixed-rate, mortgage-backed securities (MBS) guaranteed by Fannie Mae, Freddie Mac, and Ginnie Mae (referred to as "agency MBS"). The purchases were intended to lower longer-term interest rates and contribute to an overall easing of financial conditions.

The agency MBS purchase program was announced in November 2008 and the FOMC expanded the size of the program in early 2009. In total, $1.25 trillion in agency MBS were purchased between January 2009 and March 2010, when the purchase phase of the program was completed. Additional transactions were conducted after March to facilitate the settlement of the initial purchases. Outright purchases were conducted via competitive bidding to ensure that trades were executed at market rates.

Understanding the Modern Monetary System

As discussed in Chapter One, the concept of "money printing" by the Federal Reserve is a complex and confusing concept to grasp. The same is true for the way the monetary system works in the US. The Fed actually creates bank reserves and uses these reserves to purchase debt instruments at one of its member banks. It's true that the Fed finances all of its activities through money creation, sometimes referred to as "*ex nihilo*" or "out of thin air." But the Fed primarily creates this money out of thin air within the Federal Reserve Bank System and does not technically insert this fabricated money into the traditional banking system.

How money is created is likely quite different from what you believe. Fractional Reserve Banking, as taught in economic classes in years past, no longer exists.

For an interesting and detailed explanation of how our banking and monetary systems work, I turn to Cullen Roche, founder of Orcam Financial Group and author of "*Understanding the Modern Monetary System.*" For more on Mr. Roche, follow his Pragmatic Capitalism blog at www.pragcap.com, read his book of the same name and his white paper on understanding the modern monetary system. Selected excerpts from this paper follows, preceded by pertinent highlights. To read the full twenty-eight page report, visit www.nowandfutures.com or http://ssrn.com/abstract=1905625

- Banks are never reserve constrained. Banks are always capital constrained.
- In the loan creation process, banks will make loans first and will find necessary reserves after the fact.
- In recent years, the Fed has been adding reserves to the banking system in exchange for (mostly) government bonds.
- Banks lend when creditworthy customers have demand for loans. Loans create deposits, not vice versa.
- The US Fed finances all of its activities by net/new money creation, that is, *ex nihilo* money creation, "out of thin air."
- It is crucial to understand that the Fed primarily creates money in the interbank market.
- It's important to note that the Federal Reserve could, in theory, control the entire yield curve of government debt. That is, if it wanted to pin long rates at 0% there is nothing stopping it from achieving this aside from political and public backlash.

Excerpts from: "*Understanding the Modern Monetary System*" by Mr. Cullen Roche:

It's important to understand that banks are unconstrained by the government (outside of the regulatory framework) in terms of how they create money. When we go through business school we are taught that banks obtain deposits and then leverage those deposits up by 10x or so. This is why we call the modern banking system a "Fractional Reserve Banking" system. Banks supposedly lend a portion of their "reserves." There's just one problem here. **Banks are never reserve constrained**. Banks are always *capital* constrained. This can best be seen in countries such as Canada where there are no reserve requirements. Reserves are used for only two purposes – to settle payments in the interbank market and to meet the Fed's reserve requirements. Aside from this, reserves have very little impact on the day-to-day lending operations of banks in the USA. This was recently confirmed in a Fed research paper:

> "Changes in reserves are unrelated to changes in lending, and open market operations do not have a direct impact on lending. We conclude that the textbook treatment of money in the transmission mechanism can be rejected."

This point has been reinforced by Standard and Poors as well as the Bank of England in the last few years. Indeed, the mainstream does appear to be catching on to the errors of the Money Multiplier concept.

This is very important to understand because many have assumed that various Fed policies in recent years (such as Quantitative Easing) would be inflationary or even hyperinflationary. But all the Fed has been doing is adding reserves to the banking system in exchange for (mostly) government bonds. Because banks are not reserve constrained, i.e., they don't lend their reserves or multiply their reserves, this doesn't necessarily lead to more lending and will not result in the private sector being able to access more capital.

Because banks are not reserve constrained it can only mean one thing – banks lend when creditworthy customers have demand for loans (assuming the banking system is healthy and banks are engaging in the business they are designed to transact). Loans create deposits, not vice versa. Banks create new loans independent of their reserve position and the Federal Reserve is in the business of altering the composition of outstanding financial assets in an effort to maintain a target interest rate and maintaining the smoothly operating payments system that it oversees (this is part of monetary policy which only loosely impacts the direct issuance of inside money). In the loan creation process, banks will make loans first (resulting in new deposits) and will find necessary reserves after the fact (either in the overnight market or via the Fed).

Banks don't use their deposits or reserves to create loans, however. Banks make loans and find reserves after the fact if needed. But since banking is a spread business (having assets that are less expensive than liabilities) the banks will always seek the cheapest source of funds for managing their payment system. That just so happens to generally be bank deposits. This gives the appearance that banks "fund" their loan book by obtaining deposits, but this is not necessarily the case. It is better to think of banking as a spread business where the bank simply acquires the cheapest liabilities to sustain its payment system and maximize profits.

The Basic Institutional Structure of Fiat Monetary Systems

To understand the structure of the US monetary system it helps to understand why we have the system we have today. The USA was founded on the idea of a market based economy with deep skepticism towards centralized government powers. Thus, the design of the system in the USA has always remained consistent with keeping the power of money creation from being controlled entirely by the government. To the surprise of many in the mainstream and even in the field of economics, the government has far less control over the money supply than most presume. Money creation in the USA is dominated by the private banking system that competes for business (loan creation). This system designed around private money issuance has proven terribly unstable at times and in need of a stabilizing force. What has evolved over the course of hundreds of years is a complex private/public hybrid system. That system involves a complex set of public institutional structures that play a facilitating role to the private banking system.

In addition to the banking system, the monetary system of the USA includes the Treasury and the Federal Reserve. Together these two domestic monetary authorities form a facilitating currency issuer. In modern fiat money systems the government, as the legitimate representation of the people, writes the rules of the game. The term "facilitating currency issuer" is a shorthand way to denote the ability of policymakers to determine macro policies and development strategies in the process of public purpose. Understanding the institutional design of the monetary system is crucial to understanding the roles of monetary and fiscal policy within the money system. The US Treasury, for instance, is the arm of government through which fiscal policy is enacted. The Treasury enacts policy by managing the tax system and engaging in the sale of bonds in order to procure funds for spending. The Federal Reserve is an independent hybrid public/private entity that engages in monetary policy via the banking system primarily by impacting the levels of inside bank money that exist.

The Federal Reserve and How Monetary Policy Works

Monetary policy involves the use of central bank policy to influence the money supply via interest rates and other channels. The central bank enacts monetary policy primarily through influencing the amount of bank reserves in the banking system. The US Fed finances all of its activities by net/new money creation, that is, *ex nihilo* money creation, "out of thin air." But it is crucial to understand that the Fed primarily creates money in the inter-bank market. That is, the Fed can determine the amount of money within the interbank market by buying and selling securities for its own account, but does not usually inject or "print money" into the non-bank private sector as is commonly believed.

The Federal Reserve serves as the banker to the US economy, often referred to as "the lender of last resort." It can best be thought of as a clearing agent to ensure that the system of payments in the USA is always running smoothly. Since the Fed's operations run primarily through the private banking system it is often seen as only benefiting banks and no one else. But a healthy and competitive private banking system benefits us all so this goal is not necessarily misaligned with public purpose. As the primary steward of the banking system and the payments system the Fed must ensure a healthy banking system before all else.

It's important to note that the Federal Reserve could, in theory, control the entire yield curve of government debt. As the monopoly supplier of reserves there is nothing stopping the Fed from pegging the long end of the US government bond yield just as it pegs the overnight Fed Funds Rate. That is, if they wanted to pin long rates at 0% there is nothing stopping them from achieving this aside from political and public backlash. In this regard, it's important to understand that the Fed only allows the marketplace to control long rates on US Government Bonds to the degree that the Fed permits. In this sense the term "don't fight the Fed" is most appropriate since the Federal Reserve can always set the price of the instruments it buys.

Appendix Three

Resources of Interest

Charts and Financial Data - While the Internet provides a plethora of resources for financial data, charts and research, you may want to add these to your Favorites list:

<u>Trading Economics:</u> http://www.tradingeconomics.com

> This is a surprisingly resourceful website with a healthy list of charts on many topics. Be sure to poke around the tab titled "Forecast" for projections on a trove of financial data.

<u>Federal Reserve Bank of St. Louis a.k.a. FRED:</u> https://research.stlouisfed.org/fred2

> Many economists, market experts and researchers turn to the thousands of charts found at FRED for updates on key economic data. In addition to charts, they publish essays, working papers, journals and more.

Subscription Research Services - Over the past 25 years I have subscribed to numerous research and advisory services. While some advisors rely on in-house research for the majority of their professional reading, I prefer to seek out independent sources devoid of hidden agendas. Although my personal list is lengthy as

I maintain many subscriptions today, the following two are worth exploring for serious investors and financial advisors.

Lowry Research Corporation: http://lowryresearch.com

> It's funny how the basic law of supply and demand remains essential to stock market research in an age of enhanced technology and numerous "revolutionary" market advisory services. While trading fads may come and go, Lowry's has provided market research for 87 years, and its method of identifying market trends remains an essential read each week. From its website:

> "Lowry Research Corporation was founded in 1938 to provide analysts and investment professionals with an unbiased, factual analysis of the stock market. Our work is based on daily Price Change/Volume statistics of all stocks traded on the New York Stock Exchange and NASDAQ Stock Market. These tabulations are compiled each day that the Markets are open and provide the statistical foundation for our Supply vs. Demand analysis of market trends."

> It offers subscriptions for daily and weekly updates. 87 years of successful trend analysis and research is hard to pass up, I suggest you check them out.

Richard Duncan's Macro Watch: http://richardduncaneconomics. com

> It's no surprise that I remind financial advisors to check out Mr. Duncan's research. His Macro Watch program is discussed extensively in Chapter Eight. Read the dialog box for more information and be sure to note the generous discount code he extends to readers of this book. For

free access to his thoughts, visit his blog on his website, link to numerous television and radio interviews and peruse the list of books for a favorite you may enjoy.

Financial Books of Interest - Wow, the list is daunting. There are numerous terrific authors who provide interesting insight on a variety of financial topics. Some are very specific, such as books on the possible collapse of the US dollar (*The Dollar Trap* by Eswar Prasad comes to mind) or endless books on the value of owning gold (none that I strongly recommend). The following list is a good place to start, however I'm sure I omitted many excellent books. My apologies!

The Panic of 1907, by Robert F. Bruner and Sean D. Carr

The Creature from Jekyll Island, by G. Edward Griffin

Lords of Finance: The Bankers Who Broke the World, by Liaquat Ahamed

When Money Dies, by Adam Fergusson

Currency Wars: The Making of the Next Global Crisis, by James Rickards

Any book by Michael Lewis (*Boomerang*, *The Big Short*, *Liar's Poker*, etc.)

End The Fed, by Ron Paul

Stress Test: Reflections on Financial Crises, by Timothy F. Geithner

The New Depression: The Breakdown of the Paper Money Economy, by Richard Duncan

Hall of Mirrors, by Barry Eichengreen

Glossary

The majority of the following definitions were provided by Investopedia. It is a remarkable source of financial information, recognized as the largest financial education website in the world. Powered by a team of data scientists and financial experts, Investopedia offers timely, trusted and actionable financial information for every investor, from early investors to financial advisors to high net worth individuals. For the latest in financial news and information, visit www.investopedia.com.

Annuity: An annuity is a contractual financial product sold by financial institutions that is designed to accept and grow funds from an individual and then, upon annuitization, pay out a stream of payments to the individual at a later point in time. The period of time when an annuity is being funded and before payouts begin is referred to as the accumulation phase. Once payments commence, the contract is in the annuitization phase.

Asset Allocation: Asset allocation is an investment strategy that aims to balance risk and reward by apportioning a portfolio's assets according to an individual's goals, risk tolerance and investment horizon. The three main asset classes - equities, fixed-income, and cash - have different levels of risk and return, so each will behave differently over time.

Bond: A bond is a debt investment in which an investor loans money to an entity (typically corporate or governmental) which borrows the funds for a defined period of time at a variable or fixed interest rate. Bonds are used by companies, municipalities, states and sovereign governments to raise money and finance a variety of projects and activities. Owners of bonds are debtholders, or creditors, of the issuer. For a description of a Bond Ladder, see the dialog box in Chapter Six.

Bretton Woods Agreement: The Bretton Woods agreement is the landmark system for monetary and exchange rate management established in 1944. The Bretton Woods Agreement was developed at the United Nations Monetary and Financial Conference held in Bretton Woods, New Hampshire, from July 1 to July 22, 1944. Major outcomes of the Bretton Woods conference included the formation of the International Monetary Fund (IMF) and the International Bank for Reconstruction and Development and, most importantly, the proposed introduction of an adjustable pegged foreign exchange rate system. Currencies were pegged to gold and the IMF was given the authority to intervene when an imbalance of payments arose. Chapter Two discusses the Bretton Woods Agreement in greater detail.

Central Bank: A central bank is an entity responsible for overseeing the monetary system for a nation (or group of nations). Central banks have a wide range of responsibilities, from overseeing monetary policy to implementing specific goals such as currency stability, low inflation and full employment. Central banks also generally issue currency, function as the bank of the government, regulate the credit system, oversee commercial banks, manage exchange reserves and act as a lender of last resort.

Consumer Price Index (CPI): The consumer price index (CPI) is a measure that examines the weighted average of prices of a basket of consumer goods and services, such as transportation, food and medical care. The CPI is calculated by taking price changes for each item in the predetermined basket of goods and averaging them; the goods are weighted according to their importance. Changes in CPI are used to assess price changes associated with the cost of living. Sometimes referred to as "headline inflation.

Diminishing Marginal Returns: The law of diminishing marginal returns is the law of economics stating that, as the number of new employees increases, the marginal product of an additional employee will at some point be less than the marginal product of the previous employee. See Chapter Seven for an extensive discussion on this topic.

Exchange Traded Fund (ETF): An ETF, or exchange traded fund, is a marketable security that tracks an index, a commodity, bonds, or a basket of assets like an index fund. Unlike mutual funds, an ETF trades like a common stock on a stock exchange. ETFs experience price changes throughout the day as they are bought and sold. ETFs typically have higher daily liquidity and lower fees than mutual fund shares, making them an attractive alternative for individual investors. Because it trades like a stock, an ETF does not have its net asset value (NAV) calculated once at the end of every day like a mutual fund.

Fed Funds Rate: The interest rate at which a depository institution lends funds maintained at the Federal Reserve to another depository institution overnight. The federal funds rate is generally only applicable to the most creditworthy institutions when they borrow and lend overnight funds to each other. The federal funds rate is one of the most influential interest rates in the US economy, since it affects monetary and financial conditions, which in turn have a bearing on key aspects of the broad economy including employment, growth and inflation. The Federal Open Market Committee (FOMC), which is the Federal Reserve's primary monetary policymaking body, telegraphs its desired target for the federal funds rate through open market operations.

Federal Open Market Committee (FOMC): The Federal Open Market Committee (FOMC) is the branch of the Federal Reserve Board that determines the direction of monetary policy. The FOMC is composed of the board of governors, which has seven members, and five reserve bank presidents. The president of the Federal Reserve Bank of New York serves continuously, while the presidents of the other reserve banks rotate their service of one-year terms.

Fiat Money: Fiat money is currency that a government has declared to be legal tender, but is not backed by a physical commodity. The value of fiat money is derived from the relationship between supply and demand rather than the value of the material that the money is made of. Historically, most currencies were based on physical commodities such as gold or silver, but fiat money is based solely on faith. Fiat is the Latin word for "it shall be." Fiat currency is discussed further in Chapter One.

Fiscal Policy: Government spending policies that influence macroeconomic conditions. Through fiscal policy, regulators attempt to improve unemployment rates, control inflation stabilize business cycles and influence interest rates in an effort to control the economy. Fiscal policy is largely based on the ideas of British economist John Maynard Keynes (1883–1946), who believed governments could change economic performance by adjusting tax rates and government spending. See Chapter Three for more information.

Fixed-Income: Fixed-income is the colloquial name given to bonds. Fixed income is a type of investing or budgeting style for which real return rates or periodic income is received at regular intervals at reasonably predictable levels. Fixed-income budgeters and investors are often one and the same - typically retired individuals who rely on their investments to provide a regular, stable income stream. This demographic tends to invest heavily in fixed-income investments because of the reliable returns they offer.

FRED: aka Federal Reserve Bank of St. Louis website for economic data. This site offers a wealth of economic data and information to promote economic education and enhance economic research. The database is updated regularly and allows 24/7 access to regional and national financial and economic data. More at https://research.stlouisfed.org/fred2

Gold Standard: A monetary system in which a country's government allows its currency unit to be freely converted into fixed amounts of gold and vice versa. The exchange rate under the gold standard monetary system is determined by the economic difference for an ounce of gold between two currencies. The gold standard was mainly used from 1875 to 1914 and also during the interwar years.

Gross Domestic Product (GDP): Gross domestic product is the monetary value of all the finished goods and services produced within a country's borders in a specific time period. Though GDP is usually calculated on an annual basis, it can be calculated on a quarterly basis as well. GDP includes all private and public consumption, government outlays, investments and exports minus imports that occur within a defined territory. Put simply, GDP is a broad measurement of a nation's overall economic activity.

International Monetary Fund (IMF): The International Monetary Fund is an international organization created for the purpose of standardizing global financial relations and exchange rates. The IMF generally monitors the global economy, and its core goal is to economically strengthen its member countries. Specifically, the IMF was created with the intention of:

1. Promoting global monetary and exchange stability.
2. Facilitating the expansion and balanced growth of international trade.
3. Assisting in the establishment of a multilateral system of payments for current transactions.

Leveraged ETF: An exchange-traded fund (ETF) that uses financial derivatives and debt to amplify the returns of an underlying index. Leveraged ETFs are available for most indexes, such as the Nasdaq-100 and the Dow Jones Industrial Average. These funds aim to keep a constant amount of leverage during the investment time frame, such as a 2:1 or 3:1 ratio.

Monetary Policy: Monetary policy consists of the actions of a central bank, currency board or other regulatory committee that determine the size and rate of growth of the money supply, which in turn affects interest rates. Monetary policy is maintained through actions such as modifying the interest rate, buying or selling government bonds, and changing the amount of money banks are required to keep in the vault (bank reserves). The Federal Reserve is in charge of the United States' monetary policy. See Chapter Three for more information.

Mutual Fund: A mutual fund is an investment vehicle that is made up of a pool of funds collected from many investors for the purpose of investing in securities such as stocks, bonds, money market instruments and similar assets. Mutual funds are operated by money managers, who invest the fund's capital and attempt to produce capital gains and income for the fund's investors. A mutual fund's portfolio is structured and maintained to match the investment objectives stated in its prospectus.

NIRP: A negative interest rate policy (NIRP) is an unconventional monetary policy tool whereby nominal target interest rates are set with a negative value, below the theoretical lower bound of zero percent.

Operation Twist: An operation twist is the name given to a Federal Reserve monetary policy operation that involves the purchase and sale of bonds. "Operation Twist" describes a monetary process where the Fed buys and sells short-term and long-term bonds depending on its objective. For example, in September 2011, the Fed performed Operation

Twist in an attempt to lower long-term interest rates. In this operation, the Fed sold short-term Treasury bonds and bought long-term Treasury bonds, which pressured the long-term bond yields downward. For more on Operation Twist, read the dialog box in Chapter Two.

Options: An option is a financial derivative that represents a contract sold by one party (option writer) to another party (option holder). The contract offers the buyer the right, but not the obligation, to buy (call) or sell (put) a security or other financial asset at an agreed-upon price (the strike price) during a certain period of time or on a specific date (exercise date). Call options give the option to buy at a certain price, so the buyer would want the stock to go up. Put options give the option to sell at a certain price, so the buyer would want the stock to go down. For more on "writing covered calls," see the dialog box in Chapter Eight.

Plunge Protection Team (PPT): A colloquial name given to the Working Group on Financial Markets. The Plunge Protection Team was created to make financial and economic recommendations to various sectors of the economy in times of economic turbulence. The team consists of the secretary of the Treasury, the chairman of the Board of Governors of the Federal Reserve, the chairman of the SEC and the chairman of the Commodity Futures Trading Commission. For more on the PPT, see the dialog box in Chapter One.

Quantitative Easing (QE): Quantitative easing is an unconventional monetary policy in which a central bank purchases government securities or other securities from the market in order to lower interest rates and increase the money supply. Quantitative easing increases the money supply by flooding financial institutions with capital in an effort to promote increased lending and liquidity. Quantitative easing is considered when short-term interest rates are at or approaching zero, and does not involve the printing of new banknotes.

S&P500 Index: The Standard & Poor's 500 Index (S&P 500) is an index of 500 stocks chosen for market size, liquidity and industry grouping, among other factors. The S&P 500 is designed to be a leading indicator of U.S. equities and is meant to reflect the risk/return characteristics of the large cap universe.

Special Drawing Rights (SDR): Special drawing rights refer to an international type of monetary reserve currency, created by the International Monetary Fund (IMF) in 1969, which operates as a supplement to the existing reserves of member countries. Created in response to concerns about the limitations of gold and dollars as the sole means of settling international accounts, SDRs are designed to augment international liquidity by supplementing the standard reserve currencies. SDRs are discussed further in Chapter Five.

Stock: A stock is a type of security that signifies ownership in a corporation and represents a claim on part of the corporation's assets and earnings. There are two main types of stock: common and preferred. Common stock usually entitles the owner to vote at shareholders' meetings and to receive dividends. Preferred stock generally does not have voting rights, but has a higher claim on assets and earnings than the common shares. For example, owners of preferred stock receive dividends before common shareholders and have priority in the event that a company goes bankrupt and is liquidated. Stocks are also known as "shares" or "equity."

Trillion: $1 trillion is a one followed by twelve zeros, $1,000,000,000,000. If this leaves you with a blank stare and mouth slightly open, refer to the end of Chapter One for three examples to help comprehend this inconceivable . sum.

VIX: The VIX (CBOE volatility index) is the ticker symbol for the Chicago Board Options Exchange (CBOE) Volatility Index, which shows the market's expectation of 30-day volatility. It is constructed using the implied volatilities of a wide range of S&P500 index options. This volatility is meant to be forward looking and is calculated from both calls and puts. The VIX is a widely used measure of market risk and is often referred to as the "investor fear gauge."

ZIRP: Zero interest-rate policy (ZIRP) is a macroeconomic concept describing conditions with a very low nominal interest rate, such as those in present-day Japan and the United States during 2008 - 2015. ZIRP is considered to be an unconventional monetary policy instrument and can be associated with slow economic growth, deflation, and deleverage.

Acknowledgments

Live as though you'll die tomorrow, but learn as though you'll live forever.

Mahatma Gandhi

I didn't think I would have so much fun writing this book. Not only did it challenge me to delve deeper into many topics as each chapter unfolded, but people who I already respected surprised me with their valuable contributions. What started out as a good book became a great one because of them.

Economist Richard Duncan, office colleague Gregory Mallison, sister Jeanne Patrican and my wife Lisa Mattie were instrumental in elevating the quality of this publication. My years of reading economic and finance books paid off too. I found several of vital importance: *The Panic of 1907*, *The Creature from Jekyll Island*, and *Stress Test – Reflections on Financial Crises*. Finally, research from several financial journalist, most notably Robert Peston and Cullen Roche, was immensely illuminating.

Economist Richard Duncan is listed first because he primarily formed my beliefs regarding the influence of the Federal Reserve on our economy. I was first introduced to Richard when I read one of his many books. I quickly devoured it as his message was compelling and his presentation easy for me to read and understand. I was so enthralled that I gathered 55 friends and clients at a nearby restaurant in 2012 and arranged for Richard to provide a synopsis of his observations via Skype from his office in Thailand. It was a terrific event, which led me to subscribe to his *Macro Watch** video newsletter and follow his blog. He is a brilliant and insightful economist, and I am thankful for his permission to use his research and charts.

Each week in the office I can be heard saying, "Greg Mallison is the smartest guy I know!" And it's true. Not only is he and his wife, Lori, THE sought after team for any trivia contest in our tristate area, Greg has a way of sifting through the financial noise to locate the actual cause of an issue or explanation of a financial concept. As a financial advisor, his clients are fortunate to have such a gifted mind guiding their portfolios. Since 2008, I treasure our ritual of early morning meetings to discuss the finer points of the financial topic du-jour. Most of the time, the topic finds its way to the 10-Yr US Treasury yield, how money is created or how the Fed really works. Many thanks to my friend for our priceless conversations and his ability to distill complicated concepts into a few concise sentences.

When I was searching for an editor - and believe me, I needed one - I started with traditional sources. It was happenstance when I shared an early version of a chapter with my sister, Jeanne Patrican, who offered her polite, honest and direct thoughts on my writing. Voila! I found my editor. As a prolific reader, she blended her literary skills with a dose of patience as we wrestled each other over the length, depth, presentation and style of my writing. Most times she won (this is her saying that, not me). Remember, though, if you find a word out of place, it's her fault!

---

* As a professional courtesy, Richard extends a substantial discount to *Macro Watch* in Chapter Eight.

Writing this book was genuine fun and I enjoyed working late into the night and on weekends until it was finished. Problem is, I was so focused on my book that other things in my personal life suffered. Who was going to take my son to practice or my daughter to her friend's house? How about doing my share to help around the house? Enter my wife, Lisa. Once we agreed that this was something I had to do, she was a true partner and did my share of the heavy-lifting with a smile and understanding. Thanks, Love!

I have this thing about reading. If I'm waiting in line at the post office or doctor's office, I *must* have something to read. If someone were to steal all the TVs in our house, I wouldn't mind taking a few years to replace them. I'm not a big sports guy and would rather enjoy a glass of red wine with a good book. If you find yourself enjoying this book and craving more, there are many wonderful authors and books to sample. I suggest starting with the ones I mention herein, such as *The Panic of 1907* by Robert F. Bruner and Sean D. Carr, *The Creature from Jekyll Island* by G. Edward Griffin, and *Stress Test – Reflections on Financial Crises* by Timothy Geithner. I also think Michael Lewis is an excellent author and any of his books are a must for your reading list. Millions of readers obviously agree as his book, *The Big Short,* was made into a movie of the same name. *Currency Wars* by James Rickards is very well written and provides an excellent synopsis of currency manipulation and cross-border struggles. And don't forget about Richard Duncan! Start with *The New Depression: The Breakdown of the Paper Money Economy* for an excellent discussion on money creation and challenges facing our economy. Keep a highlighter handy, as there are many gems within the book worth re-reading. Appendix Three provides additional resources of interest.

Finally, the Internet allowed me to stumble upon the excellent journalism of Robert Peston, formally of the BBC and now Political Editor for ITV News. Over the years, I enjoyed BBC reporting and it remains a preset favorite on Sirius radio in my car. No commercials are an added bonus! Finally, as Greg saw my deepening interest in how money is actually created, he directed me to a detailed white paper on the topic from Cullen Roche, author of *Understanding the Modern Monetary System*. For a deep dive into the complexities of this topic, to debunk the theory of Fractional Reserve Banking and more, read Cullen's work and follow his *Pragmatic Capitalism* blog. Appendix Two attempts to enlighten readers on this intricate topic.